Department of Health and Welsh Office

Mental Health Act 1983

Memorandum on Parts I to VI, VIII and X

London: The Stationery Office

Second impression 1998

Acknowledgement
With thanks to Richard Jones of Morgan Bruce, Solicitors for his extensive advice and support in producing this edition of the memorandum.

NHS Executive
Department of Health

Mental Health Act 1983
Explanatory memorandum on Parts I, II, III, IV, V, VI, VIII and X of the Act and associated Schedules, and on the Mental Health (Hospital, Guardianship and Consent to Treatment) Regulations 1983.
ISBN 0 11 322112 6

Contents

Part IV   Consent to treatment

Part V   Mental Health Review Tribunals

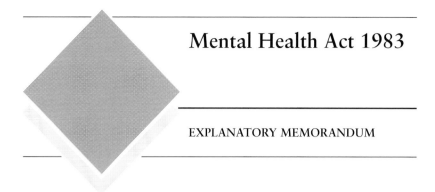

Mental Health Act 1983

EXPLANATORY MEMORANDUM

Introduction

1   This Memorandum, which describes the main provisions of the Mental Health Act 1983, (the Act) is for the guidance of all those who work with the Act. It cannot provide an authoritative interpretation of the law or override the statutory provisions of the Act and regulations. Nor does it describe every detail of the Act, Regulations and Rules which must be referred to when necessary. It does not cover Part VII of the Act which deals with the management of the property and affairs of patients and the Court of Protection, or Part IX which deals with offences.

2   The Act, which has been amended by subsequent legislation (see appendix 6) is divided into ten Parts and six schedules. It can be seen from the table of contents that this Memorandum generally follows the order in which provisions appear in the Act. Except where specified, references to Parts, sections and schedules in this Memorandum are references to Parts, sections and schedules of the Mental Health Act 1983, and references to regulations are references to the Mental Health (Hospital, Guardianship and Consent to Treatment) Regulations 1983. These Regulations have also been amended by subsequent legislation. References to decisions of the High Court on the interpretation of the Act are made throughout the text.

Code of Practice

3   The Code of Practice provides guidance to practitioners and others on how they should proceed when undertaking duties under the Act and should be read in conjunction with the Memorandum.

Interpretations

4　Many of the definitions used in the Act are to be found in section 145(1). However, these may be varied in certain Parts of the Act, and where this happens the definitions that apply may usually be found in the interpretation section of that Part, or in the section itself. For example, a general definition of 'local social services authority' is given in section 145(1), but a more limited definition is given in section 117(3) where the particular local social services authority on which the duty is placed is indicated.

5　The following interpretations are particularly important:

a.　**'Hospital'** The definition of hospital in the Act covers all hospitals in the National Health Service (including Special Hospitals) Any such hospital may admit and detain patients under the procedures laid down in the Act. For most of the Act's purposes the definition of hospital also includes a mental nursing home which is registered to care for detained patients under the Registered Homes Act 1984. The definition of mental nursing home in the 1984 Act covers small specialist units to large private psychiatric hospitals.

b.　**'The Managers'** In relation to National Health Service hospitals 'the managers' means the NHS trust, Health Authority or Special Health Authority which administers the hospital; for high security hospitals it means the Secretary of State who has delegated this role to Special Health Authorities and for mental nursing homes it means the person or persons registered in respect of the home under the Registered Homes Act 1984 (see section 145).

c.　**'The responsible medical officer'** The responsible medical officer is defined in section 34(1) as the registered medical practitioner in charge of a detained patient's treatment. In relation to guardianship the responsible medical officer is the registered medical practitioner authorised by the responsible local social services authority to act as responsible medical officer, for a specific purpose or generally (see paras 60 and 61).

d.　**'The nearest relative'** The terms 'relative' and 'nearest relative' are defined in section 26 (see para 62).

e. **'Approved social workers'** The functions given under the Act to approved social workers may only be carried out by officers of local social services authorities approved and appointed for this purpose.

f. 'Patient' A patient is a person suffering from or appearing to suffer from mental disorder (there is a different interpretation of patient in Part VII of the Act, see section 94).

g. **'Medical treatment'** Medical treatment is defined as including 'nursing ..... care, habilitation and rehabilitation under medical supervision' (see section 145).

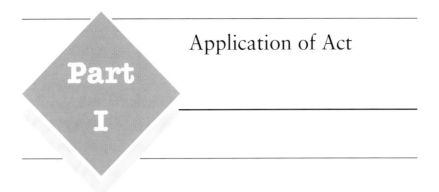

Application of Act

Application of the Act *(section 1)*

6   The Act concerns 'the reception, care and treatment of mentally disordered patients, the management of their property and other related matters' (section 1(1)). 'Mental disorder is defined as 'mental illness, arrested or incomplete development of mind, psychopathic disorder and any other disorder or disability of mind'

Definitions of mental illness, mental impairment, severe mental impairment and psychopathic disorder

7   For most purposes of the Act - which are more fully set out below - it is not enough for a patient to be suffering from any mental disorder as defined above; he must be suffering from one or more of the four specific categories of mental disorder set out in the Act - mental illness, mental impairment, severe mental impairment or psychopathic disorder.

8   The term **'mental illness'**[1] is undefined, and its operational definition and usage is a matter for clinical judgement in each case. The terms **'mental impairment'** and **'severe mental impairment'** are used in the Act where learning disability is associated with abnormally aggressive or seriously irresponsible conduct. These terms are intended to distinguish the small minority of people with learning disabilities who need to be detained in hospital or received into guardianship, from the great majority who do not.

---

[1] (The High Court has confirmed that anorexia nervosa is a mental illness for the purpose of the Act (Re K B (Adult) (Mental Patient: Medical Treatment (1994) 19 BMLR 144).

9   The definition of 'mental impairment' has two main components. First, it refers to 'a state of arrested or incomplete development of mind which includes significant impairment of intelligence and social functioning'. Secondly there is the qualification that the learning disability must be associated with 'abnormally aggressive or seriously irresponsible' conduct. This is intended to ensure that people with learning disabilities are not subject to long-term compulsory powers unless the behaviour which is part of their condition in that particular case justifies the use of those powers.

10   The distinction between 'severe mental impairment' and 'mental impairment' is one of degree: the impairment of intelligence and social functioning is 'severe' in the former and only 'significant' in the latter. Slight impairment cannot fall within either definition. The assessment of the level of impairment is a matter for clinical judgement. This distinction between the two degrees of mental impairment is important because there are differences in the grounds on which patients can be detained, or have their detention renewed if they suffer from severe mental impairment as opposed to mental impairment (paras 20, 66, 97, 150, 157, 158, 167, 193, 201, 204 and 240 below).

11   **Psychopathic** disorder must be a persistent disorder or disability; in other words there must have been signs that the disorder has existed for a considerable period before a patient can be classified as having psychopathic disorder. It must result in abnormally aggressive or seriously irresponsible conduct.

12   As with mental impairment the **treatability** of the condition is not mentioned in the definition. However, the effect of sections 3, 37 and 47 are that those with psychopathic disorder (or mental impairment) cannot be compulsorily admitted to hospital for treatment unless it can be stated that medical treatment is likely to alleviate or prevent a deterioration of their condition.

Exclusions from the definitions of mental disorder

13 Section 1(3) of the Act states that a person may not be dealt with under the Act as suffering from mental disorder purely by reason of promiscuity, other immoral conduct, sexual deviance or dependence on alco-

hol or drugs. This means that there are no grounds for detaining a person in hospital because of alcohol or drug abuse alone, but it is recognized that alcohol or drug abuse may be accompanied by or associated with mental disorder. It is therefore possible to detain a person who is dependent on alcohol or drugs if he or she is suffering from a mental disorder arising from or suspected to arise from alcohol or drug dependence or from the withdrawal of alcohol or a drug, if all the other relevant conditions are met. Similarly sexual deviancy is not of itself a mental disorder, for the purposes of the Act, which can provide grounds for compulsory detention.

Part II
Compulsory Admission to Hospital and Guardianship

Introduction

14   Part II of the Act deals with the circumstances in which, and procedures through which, patients may be compulsorily admitted to and detained in hospital or received into guardianship, otherwise than through the Courts, or on transfer from prison or other institutions (Part III) or on return to the United Kingdom (Part VI). It also provides for the aftercare under supervision of certain categories of detained patients when they leave hospital.

Admission for assessment *(section 2)*

15   Admission to and detention in hospital for assessment under section 2 may be authorised where a patient is (a) suffering from mental disorder of a nature or degree which warrants the detention of the patient in hospital for assessment (or for assessment followed by medical treatment) for at least a limited period and (b) he ought to be so detained in the interests of his health or safety, or with a view to the protection of others. Detention is for up to 28 days. The words in brackets make it clear that a patient detained under section 2 may be given treatment other than assessment procedures (but see paras 212 to 230). It is envisaged that many patients will complete their treatment in hospital within a period of detention under section 2 and can then be discharged. Others may stay as informal patients or, if they satisfy the conditions, they can be detained under section 3 for longer term treatment.

Admission for treatment *(section 3)*

16   The grounds for admission for treatment are firstly that the patient is suffering from one or more of the four forms of mental disorder set out in Part I of the Act - mental illness, mental impairment, severe mental impairment and psychopathic disorder (see paras 7 to 13). Unlike section 2, a finding that the patient is merely suffering from a 'mental disorder' is not sufficient. Secondly, the mental disorder must be of a nature or degree which makes it appropriate for the patient to receive medical treatment in hospital. Section 3 cannot therefore be used if the intention is to admit and detain the patient for a purely nominal period during which no necessary treatment will be given (R v Hallstrom ex p. W; R v Gardner, ex p. L (1986) 2 All ER 306). Thirdly, for a patient suffering from psychopathic disorder or mental impairment there is an additional condition that medical treatment is likely to alleviate or prevent a deterioration in the patient's condition. Treatment need not be expected to cure the patient's disorder: the condition is satisfied if, in the opinion of the doctors making the medical recommendations, medical treatment is likely to enable the patient to cope more satisfactorily with his disorder or its symptoms, or if it stops his condition from becoming worse. Because the interpretation of medical treatment is a wide one, this condition would be satisfied if, for example, a psychopathic or mentally impaired patient would benefit from care, habilation or rehabilitation under medical supervision in a hospital. Fourthly, it must be necessary for the health *or* safety of the patient *or* for the protection of others that he should receive this treatment, and it cannot be provided unless he is detained under section 3.

Applications for admission to hospital

17   Section 11 sets out the general provisions for applications for admission for treatment, assessment or guardianship (dealt with in paras 32-36). An application for admission must be made by either the patient's nearest relative (see para 63), or an approved social worker (see para 5(e)). An application must be addressed to the managers of the hospital to which admission is sought and must state the qualification of the applicant to make the application. An application for admission for assessment or treatment must be accompanied by written recommendations from two medical practitioners. One of these must be approved under section 12(2) of the Act as having special experience in the diagnosis and

treatment of mental disorder. Circular HSG(96)3 (for Wales PSM(96)(3)) 'Approval of doctors under section 12 of the Mental Health Act 1983' gives advice to Health Authorities about the approval of such medical practitioners. One of them should, if practicable, know the patient personally.

18   The procedures for making an application and recording an admission are laid down in regulation 4 of the Mental Health (Hospital, Guardianship and Consent to Treatment) Regulations 1983. Applications must be served by delivering them to an officer of the managers of the hospital to which admission is sought who is authorised to receive them (regulation 3(2)). This means that in practice the document should be delivered to the hospital that is authorised to detain the patient.

Applications for admission for assessment under section 2

19   In the case of admission for assessment both medical recommendations must state that, in the opinion of the practitioner, the patient is suffering from mental disorder of a nature or degree which warrants his detention in a hospital for assessment (or for assessment followed by medical treatment) for at least a limited period, and that he ought to be detained in the interests of his own health or safety or for the protection of other persons. A specific diagnosis of the form of mental disorder is not required, as part of the purpose of the 'assessment' may be to determine this. However, the words 'of a nature or degree which warrants (his) detention in a hospital' are intended to restrict the use of the section to patients who are thought to be suffering from a form of mental disorder which would justify admission under the Act. The conditions for section 2 admissions are not quite so stringent as those for section 3 admissions because assessment may well be used for the purpose of determining whether the more stringent conditions for admission for treatment are met. The powers under section 2 can only be used for the limited purpose for which they were intended, and cannot be utilised for the purpose of further detaining a patient for the purposes of assessment beyond the 28 days period, or used as a stop-gap procedure while an application is made to the county court under section 29 for an order to appoint an acting nearest relative (R v Wilson , ex p. Williamson [1996] C.O.D. 42. and see paras 107 and 108). The forms of application and recommendations for section 2 are Forms 1-4.

Applications for admission for treatment under section 3

20   The medical recommendations for an admission for treatment must state that, in the opinion of both the medical practitioners, the conditions set out in para 16 are satisfied. The particulars must set out the following details which are prescribed in regulations: the form or forms of disorder from which the patient suffers (both medical recommendations must contain one form of disorder in common); the reasons why the patient cannot suitably be cared for outside of hospital, or be treated as an out-patient, or be admitted as an informal patient; and, in the case of a patient suffering from psychopathic disorder or mental impairment, the reason why treatment is likely to alleviate or prevent a deterioration in his condition. (Form 10 or 11)

Medical recommendations

21   The following requirements apply in general to medical recommendations for the purposes of Part II:

i.   Where the two medical practitioners examine the patient separately, not more than five days must have elapsed between the days on which separate examinations took place (section 12(1)).

ii.   One of the practitioners should be approved for the purposes of section 12(2).

iii. One of the practitioners should, if practicable, have had previous acquaintance with the patient.

iv.   Except in the cases mentioned below, only one medical recommendation may come from a practitioner on the staff of the hospital to which the patient is to be admitted. This does not apply to a patient to be admitted to a mental nursing home or as a private patient in an NHS hospital, when neither recommendation may come from a doctor on the staff. Section 12(6) states that a general practitioner who is employed part -time in a hospital does not count for the purposes of the section as a practitioner on its staff. This means that medical recommendations can be given by, for example, a full-time consultant psychiatrist and the patient's GP even if the GP happens to work part -time in the hospital in question.

22 The Act makes provision for the practical difficulties which may arise in obtaining two medical recommendations in cases of emergency or urgency: for example, where a Health Authority has comparatively few approved doctors. Both medical recommendations may come from medical practitioners on the staff of the hospital concerned, subject to the following conditions (sub-sections 3 and 4 of section 12):

- fulfilling the conditions set out above would cause delay involving serious risk to the health or safety of the patient; and
- one of the two doctors concerned works at the hospital for less than half the time for which he is bound by contract to work for the NHS; and
- where one recommendation is made by a consultant the other may not be made by a doctor who works under him.

23 Recommendations may only be given by two doctors on the staff of the same hospital if all three of these conditions are satisfied. Usually the recommendations will be from the patient's GP and the consultant who will be his responsible medical officer. A medical practitioner, in making any medical recommendation, is responsible for the information which he provides in connection with the application.

Admission for assessment in cases of emergency

24 In exceptional cases it may be necessary to admit a patient for assessment as an emergency without obtaining a second medical recommendation. An emergency application may be made by an approved social worker or by the nearest relative of the patient, and must state that it is of urgent necessity that the patient should be admitted and detained for assessment, and that compliance with the normal procedures would involve undesirable delay. Only one medical recommendation is required but the practitioner concerned must have seen the patient within the previous *24 hours* (see para 51). Similarly, the applicant must have seen the patient in the previous *24 hours*. Forms 5-7 are used for emergency applications. The form for the medical recommendation asks for certain information to clarify the circumstances of the emergency, which may be required by hospital managers or the Mental Health Act Commission.

The recommendation (on form 7) should preferably be given by a practitioner who has had previous acquaintance with the patient. The application is effective for 72 hours in which time a second medical recommendation must be obtained in accordance with the requirements of section 12 (with the exception of the requirement as to the time of the second signature). If the second recommendation is received during that period the patient may be detained for 28 days from admission as if originally admitted under section 2.

Applications in respect of patients already in hospital

25 An application for 'admission' (in other words compulsory detention) under section 2 or 3 may be made in respect of patients who are already in hospital as informal patients. An informal patient may also be detained for up to 72 hours under section 5(2) if the doctor in charge of his treatment reports that an application for admission under section 2 or 3 ought to be made. This report should be made on form 12 and should be given immediately to an officer authorised to receive such reports on behalf of the managers (see para 59). The 72 hour period begins to run from the time the report is delivered to the officer.

26 It may occasionally be necessary to make a report under section 5(2) in respect of a patient who is not in a psychiatric hospital or the psychiatric wing of a general hospital. Where a patient is receiving psychiatric treatment (even though he may also be receiving non-psychiatric treatment) the doctor in charge of the treatment for the purposes of section 5(2) will be the consultant or senior psychiatrist concerned. But where an in-patient is not receiving psychiatric treatment, the doctor who is in charge of the treatment the patient is receiving would have power to furnish the report. Where such a report is made by a non-psychiatrist, a senior psychiatrist should see the patient as soon as possible to determine whether the patient should be detained further.

27 Section 5(3) provides that the medical practitioner in charge of a patient's treatment may nominate (ie name) one, but only one, other medical practitioner on the staff of the same hospital to act on his behalf under the section, in his absence. A nurse of the prescribed class may also detain an informal patient for up to 6 hours under strictly specified circumstances (see para 28).

Nurse's six hour holding power (section 5(4))

28 A nurse who is qualified to nurse patients suffering from mental illness or learning disabilities (see the Mental Health (Nurses) Order 1983[1]), may detain an informal patient **who is already being treated for mental disorder,** for up to six hours if it appears to him that:

i. the patient is suffering from mental disorder to such a degree that it is necessary for his health or safety, or for the protection of others, for him to be immediately restrained from leaving the hospital; and

ii. it is not practicable to secure the immediate attendance of a medical practitioner for the purpose of furnishing a report under section 5(2).

29 The holding power starts after the nurse has recorded his opinion on the prescribed form (form 13) and ends either six hours later, or on the earlier arrival of one of the two doctors entitled to make such a report under section 5(2). The doctor is free either to make such a report or to decide not to detain the patient further (which may, for example, include persuading him to stay voluntarily). The written record made by the nurse must be delivered to the hospital managers, or someone authorized to act on their behalf (see para 59), as soon as possible either by the nurse or by someone authorised by the nurse. The nurse, or another nurse of the prescribed class, should also take steps to let the managers know as soon as the power has lapsed by delivering form 16 to them in the same way. The six hour holding period counts as part of the 72 hours if the doctor concerned decides to make a report under section 5(2).

Duty to inform nearest relative (section 11)

30 Section 11(3) requires an approved social worker (see para 5(e)) who makes an application for admission for assessment to take whatever steps are practicable to inform the person, if any, appearing to be the patient's nearest relative that the application is about to be or has been made and of the relative's power to discharge the patient. The actual giving of the information need not necessarily be undertaken by the approved social worker who made the application (R v South Western Hospital Managers, ex p. M. [1994] 1 ALL E.R. 161). In the case of an application for admission for treatment or for guardianship the approved social worker

---

1 This will be replaced by a new Order in 1998.

should try to consult the nearest relative prior to making the application (section 11(4)). The consultation with the nearest relative can precede the obtaining of the two medical recommendations (Re Whitbread (Times Law Report) 14 July 1997) and in suitable circumstances the approved social worker can carry out his duty to consult through the medium of another (R v South Western Hospital Managers, ex p. M. [1994] 1 All ER 161). If the nearest relative objects, the approved social worker cannot proceed, but an unreasonable objection by a relative is one of the grounds in section 29(3) for a court to transfer the powers of the nearest relative to another person. The Act recognises that it may not always be possible for the approved social worker to identify or to contact the nearest relative (see para 32).

Transport of a patient to hospital

31   An application for admission, including the appropriate medical recommendation or recommendations, are sufficient authority for the compulsory removal by the applicant or by anyone authorized by him of a patient to the hospital named in the application and his detention there. The authority to remove to hospital expires 14 days after the last medical examination for the purposes of a medical recommendation. In the case of an emergency application the period is 24 hours from the medical examination, or the time when the application was made, whichever is earlier. Where it is necessary to provide transport to take the patient to hospital, this comes within the duty of Health Authorities and NHS trusts to provide ambulance services. If the patient is likely to be unwilling to be moved, the applicant should provide the ambulance attendant or escort with written authority. If the patient absconds while being taken to hospital he may be retaken within the 14 days or 24 hour period, whichever applies (see paras 70-80, sections 6, 137 and 138 and regulation 9).

Duty of approved social workers to make applications for admission or for guardianship *(section 13)*

32   Section 13 lays on an approved social worker a duty to make an application for admission or guardianship (see paras 38-42) in any case where he considers an application ought to be made and where, after taking into account the views of the relatives and any other relevant circumstances he thinks it necessary and proper to do so. This does not affect the provisions as to consultation with nearest relatives mentioned

above (see para 30), but, subject to those provisions, and the powers of the nearest relatives, it lays on approved social workers a duty to act when necessary, particularly if relatives are unable or unwilling to do so. The nearest relative may often prefer that the approved social worker should sign an application. The person making the application must have seen the patient within a period of 14 days ending with the date of signing the application (24 hours for emergency applications for admission for assessment.) (sections 11(5) and 4(2)).

33   Although an approved social worker must have regard to a recent decision, if any, of a Mental Health Review Tribunal discharging a patient from detention, such a decision does not restrict the duty of the approved social worker to make an application if the provisions of section 13 are satisfied (R v South Western Hospital Managers, ex p. M. [1994] 1 All E.R. 161).

34   Section 13(2) requires the approved social worker to interview the patient 'in a suitable manner' - e.g. taking account of any hearing or linguistic difficulties the patient may have. He must also satisfy himself that detention in a hospital is the most appropriate way of providing the care and medical treatment the patient needs. He is required to consider 'all the circumstances' of the case: these will include the past history of the patient's mental disorder, his present condition and the social, familiar, and personal factors bearing on it, the wishes of the patient and his relatives, and medical opinion. To do this he will need to consult all those professionally involved in the case (for example the doctor or a community psychiatric nurse) and the patient's main carer(s). In order to assess the available options the approved social worker will have to inform himself as to the availability and suitability of other means of giving the patient care and medical treatment, such as treatment as an informal patient, day care, out- patient treatment, community psychiatric nursing support, crisis intervention centres, primary health care support, local authority social services provision, and support from friends, relatives and voluntary organisations.

35   Section 13(3) provides that an approved social worker may make an application outside the area of the local social services authority he works for. This might be necessary if, for example, a patient is admitted informally to a hospital outside his local authority and then needs to be de-

tained. In such a case it would be desirable for an approved social worker from the local authority in which the patient is normally resident to make the application for an assessment even though the patient is technically the responsibility of the local authority in which the hospital is situated .

36   Section 13(4) enables the nearest relative to require the social services authority in whose area the patient resides to direct an approved social worker to consider applying for a patient's admission to hospital. If he decides not to make the application he must inform the relative of his reasons in writing.

Social report *(section 14)*

37   Section 14 provides that when a patient is compulsorily admitted to hospital following an application by his nearest relative, the managers must inform the local social services authority in the area where the patient lived before admission. As soon as practicable the authority must then arrange for a social worker to interview the patient and provide a report on the patient's social circumstances which should be sent to the hospital managers. (This should cover the areas described in para 34.)

Guardianship

38   Placing a mentally disordered person under guardianship enables the guardian to exercise certain powers which are set out in section 8. The guardian may be the local social services authority, or an individual approved by the local social services authority, such as a relative of the patient. In most cases it should be possible for patients for whom care in the community is appropriate to receive that care without being subjected to the control of guardianship. However, in a minority of cases guardianship enables a relative or social worker to help a mentally disordered person to manage in the community where the alternative would be admission to hospital. Patients may only be received into guardianship if they have reached the age of 16 years.

The grounds for guardianship

39   The grounds for guardianship are that the patient is suffering from mental illness, mental impairment, severe mental impairment or psychopathic disorder and guardianship must be necessary 'in the interests of the welfare of the patient or for the protection of other persons'. The

purpose of guardianship is therefore primarily to ensure that the patient receives care and protection rather than medical treatment, although the guardian does have powers to require the patient to attend for medical treatment (but not to make him accept treatment). A guardianship application must be founded on two medical recommendations, the procedure being similar to an application for admission for treatment (see para 20 regulation 5) (Forms 17-20).

Powers of a guardian

40   The effect of a guardianship application, if accepted, is to give the guardian three specific powers as set down in section 8(1). The first power is to require the patient to live at the place specified by the guardian. This may be used to discourage the patient from sleeping rough or living with people who may exploit or mistreat him, or to ensure that he resides in a particular hostel or other facility. The second power enables the guardian to require the patient to attend specified places at specified times for medical treatment, occupation, education or training. These might include a local authority day centre, or a hospital, surgery or clinic. The third power enables the guardian to require access to the patient to be given at the place where the patient is living, to any doctor, approved social worker, or other person specified by the guardian. This power could be used, for example, to ensure that the patient did not neglect himself. Section 18 provides that if without his guardian's consent, a patient leaves the place where he is required by his guardian to live, he may be taken into custody and returned within the period set out in section 18(4) (see paras 70-80). A patient under guardianship may also be transferred to hospital (see para 91-92).

Applications for guardianship

41   The application and recommendations for reception into guardianship must be forwarded to the local social services authority named as the proposed guardian, or to the local social services authority in whose area the proposed guardian lives. An application may not be made if the nearest relative objects (section 11(4)). The guardianship application, and the guardian, if a private individual, must be accepted by this authority. Form 21 should be used to record acceptance and this form should be attached to the application (regulation 5(3)). Similarly, the receipt of medical recommendations must be recorded on form 15. If the applica-

tion is accepted the authority will become 'the responsible local social services authority' (section 34(3)) holding the power of discharge under section 23 and with duties of visiting and supervision under regulation 13. When the guardian is a private individual it will no doubt be usual for the patient to live with him or near to him, but if the patient lives temporarily or permanently in another area, the responsible social services authority is the authority in whose area the guardian lives. Similarly, where a local social services authority is the guardian, it may arrange for the patient to live, temporarily or permanently, outside its own area but so long as that authority remains guardian it remains responsible for visiting and supervision. If the new living arrangement is likely to be permanent, consideration should be given to transferring the guardianship under section 19 to the local social services authority for the area where the patient is residing.

42   If the proposed guardian is not the local social services authority, the application should be accompanied by a written statement from the proposed guardian that he is willing to act as guardian (to be set out in Part II of form 17 or 18). The application does not take effect until it is accepted by the local social services authority. When accepted it confers the powers and duties of guardian on the guardian from the date of acceptance. The local social services authority should consider the suitability of any proposed guardian before accepting the application. Any guardian should be a person who can appreciate any special disabilities and needs of a mentally disordered person and who will look after the patient in an appropriate and sympathetic way. The guardian should display an interest in promoting the patient's physical and mental health and in providing for his occupation, training, employment, recreation and general welfare in a suitable way. The local social services authority must satisfy itself that the proposed guardian is capable of carrying out his functions and should assist the guardian with advice and other facilities. Regulation 12 provides that they can call for reports and information from the guardian, as they may require; the guardian also has a duty to inform them of his address, the address of the patient and of the nominated medical attendant, and if the patient should die.

Nominated medical attendant

43   Regulation 12 requires the guardian, if not a local social services authority, to appoint a doctor to act as the 'nominated medical attendant' who will care for the patient's general health. This doctor has the power to reclassify the patient (section 16) and is responsible for examining the patient when the authority for his guardianship is due to expire and for making a report renewing the guardianship, if appropriate (section 20). It is for the guardian to decide who to appoint as the nominated medical attendant, but this should be done after consultation with the local social services authority. The medical attendant may be the patient's general practitioner. When the guardian is a social services authority these functions are carried out by the responsible medical officer defined in paragraph 5(c) above. The responsible medical officer has the power of discharge in all cases (see para 106). It is for the local social services authority to decide who is to act as the responsible medical officer, either generally for a particular patient, or on a specific occasion. The responsible local social services authority should wherever practicable nominate a consultant psychiatrist who has been involved in the patient's treatment.

Scrutiny and rectification of documents

44   The people who sign the applications and make the medical recommendations should make sure that they comply with the requirements of the Act. Those who act on the authority of these documents should also make sure that they are in the proper form, as an incorrectly completed form may not constitute authority for a patient's detention. Section 15 of the Act contains provisions under which documents which are found to be incorrect, defective or insufficient may be rectified after they have been acted on. Patients may continue to be detained for a limited period while an error capable of rectification is corrected.

Faulty applications

45   Admission documents should be carefully scrutinised as soon as the patient has been admitted, or, if he is already in hospital, as soon as the documents are received. The managers of the hospital should nominate an officer to undertake this task (see para 58 and regulation 4(2)). The local social services authority should also appoint an officer to receive

and scrutinise documents submitted in support of applications for guardianship (regulation 5(2)). The following kinds of faults should be looked for:

a. those which invalidate the application completely and cannot be rectified

b. those which may be amended under section 15 - in particular those which make a medical recommendation insufficient to warrant the detention of the patient, but which may be capable of rectification by the substitution of a new medical recommendation under subsections (2) and (3) of section 15.

Faults which invalidate the application

46   Documents cannot be rectified under section 15 unless they are documents which can properly be regarded as applications or medical recommendations within the meaning of the Act. A document cannot be regarded as an application or medical recommendation if it is not signed at all or is signed by a person who is not empowered to do so under the Act. This means that a check should be made to confirm that an application is signed by the patient's nearest relative or the acting nearest relative or an approved social worker; and that each medical recommendation is signed by a practitioner who is not excluded under section 12. In doing so the officer scrutinising the form may take statements at face value; for example, he need not check that the doctor who states he is a registered medical practitioner is registered (regulation 3(4)). Another fault which would invalidate the application completely would be if the two medical recommendations did not specify at least one form of mental disorder in common (section 11(6)).

47   If any fault of this sort is discovered there is no authority for the patient's detention because rectification under section 15 cannot be used to enable a fundamentally defective application to be retrospectively validated (Re S-C (Mental Patient: Habeas Corpus)[1996] 1 All ER 532). In these circumstances authority for the patient's detention can only be obtained through a new application. If the patient is already in hospital he can only be detained if the medical practitioner in charge of his treatment (or his nominee) issues a report under section 5 of the Act. Any new application must, of course, be accompanied by medical recommenda-

tions which comply with the Act but this does not exclude the possibility of one of the two existing medical recommendations being used if the time limits and other provisions of the Act can still be complied with (sections 6, 11 and 12).

Errors which may be amended under section 15

48   Section 15 allows an application or medical recommendation which is found to be in any respect incorrect or defective to be amended by the person who signed it, with the consent of the managers of the hospital, within the period of 14 days from the date of the patient's admission. Faults which may be capable of amendment under this section include the leaving blank of any spaces on the form which should have been filled in (other than the signature) or failure to delete one or more alternatives in places where only one can be correct. The patient's forenames and surname should agree in all the places where they appear in the application and supporting recommendations.

49   Any document found to contain faults of this sort should be returned to the person who signed it for amendment. When the amended document is returned to the hospital it should again be scrutinised to check that it is now in the proper form. Consent to the amendment should then be given by an officer of the hospital or mental nursing home who has been authorised to consent to amendments on behalf of the managers (regulation 4(2)). In the case of mental nursing homes, the managers, if two or more in number, may authorise one of their number to consent to amendments. These officers can also issue notices under section 15(2). Similarly, a local social services authority may authorise in writing an officer or class of officers to carry out these functions (regulation 5(2)). The consent should be recorded in writing and could take the form of an endorsement on the document itself. If this is all done within a period of 14 days starting with the date on which the patient was admitted (or the date when the documents were received if the patient was already in hospital when the application was made) the documents are deemed to have had effect as though originally made as amended.

Time limits for medical recommendations

50   Another point which should be checked as soon as the documents are first received is whether the time limits mentioned in sections 6, 11

and 12 have been complied with. Except for emergency applications under section 4, these limits are:

a.   the date on which the applicant last saw the patient must be within the period of 14 days ending with the date of the application;

b.   the dates of the medical *examinations* of the patient by the two doctors who gave the recommendations (not the dates of the recommendations themselves) must be not more than 5 clear days apart (ie if one examination took place on 1 January the other can take place no later than 7 January);

c.   the dates of signatures of both medical recommendations must not be later than the date of the application;

d.   the patient's admission to hospital (or if the patient is already in hospital the reception of the documents by a person authorised by the hospital managers to receive them) must take place within 14 days beginning with the date of the later of the two medical examinations.

51   When an emergency application is made under section 4 it is accompanied in the first place by only one medical recommendation. The time limits which apply to emergency applications are:

a.   the time at which the applicant last saw the patient must be within the period of 24 hours ending with the time of the application;

b.   the patient's admission to hospital must take place within the period of 24 hours starting with the time of the medical examination or with the time of the application whichever is earlier. An emergency application may be signed either before or after the medical recommendation;

c.   the second medical recommendation must be received on behalf of the managers not more than 72 hours after the time of the patient's admission. The two medical recommendations must then comply with all the normal requirements except the requirement as to the time of the signature of the second recommendation.

Faulty medical recommendations

52   If the dates entered on the application and medical recommenda-

tions do not conform with these time limits the persons who signed them should be asked whether the dates or times entered are correct. If they are not correct and the correct dates or times do conform with the limits the entry on the forms may be amended under section 15(1). If the time limits have not been complied with, then the application is invalid unless it is capable of rectification by the substituting of a new medical recommendation under section 15(3).

53   It will be noted that notice of the rejection of a recommendation under section 15(2) must be sent in writing to the applicant (whereas a request for amendment under section 15(1) should be sent direct to the person who signed the document in question). It would be advisable at the same time to inform the doctor who gave the recommendation. The applicant - especially when not an approved social worker- should be advised that he may submit a fresh recommendation within the 14 days from the patient's admission. In some cases it may be suitable for the fresh recommendation to be given by a doctor on the staff of the hospital.

54   Section 15(3) allows the procedure described in sub-section (2) to be used when both recommendations are good in themselves but taken together are insufficient, for example, when neither is given by a doctor approved under section 12, or when the time limits applying to medical examinations mentioned in para 50-51 above have not been complied with. In such cases either recommendation may be replaced by a fresh one under section 15(2). But this procedure may not be used if the recommendations do not comply with the requirement in section 12 that they must agree in specifying at least one form of mental disorder in common, as mentioned in para 46 and 47 above.

Approved medical practitioners

55   Another point to be checked in all cases is whether one of the two medical recommendations is given by a practitioner who is approved by the Secretary of State under section 12(2). Each doctor is required to state in the medical recommendation whether or not he is so approved. The statement can be taken at face value if there is no reason to suspect falsification, but if neither recommendation states that the doctor is approved, enquiries should be made. If in fact one of these doctors is approved, the statement or the recommendation may be amended under

section 15. If neither doctor is approved, but the recommendations are otherwise in proper form, a new recommendation must be sought under section 15(3).

The managers of hospitals

56   The definition of the 'managers' of a hospital or mental nursing home is covered in paragraph 5(b) above. The power to detain patients admitted under the Act rests with the managers (section 6(2) and section 40(1)) and they, amongst others, have powers of discharge (section 23(2) and 23(3)). Various reports and notices must be given to them, and they have other powers and duties which are described elsewhere in this Memorandum. In particular, they have responsibilities for the referral of certain cases to a Mental Health Review Tribunal (section 68) (see paras 234 and 246) and for withholding patients' correspondence in certain cases (section 134) (see paras 303 -310). They must also ensure that patients, and where possible their nearest relatives, are informed of their rights (section 132), (see paras 297-301) and that the nearest relative is informed of a patient's discharge (section 133) (see para 302). All the functions mentioned above may be performed on behalf of the managers by members or officers where authorised to do so in accordance with the Act and regulations.

57   There are specific provisions with regard to the discharge of patients. Section 23(4) allows the manager's power of discharge to be exercised by any three or more members (not officers) authorised by them to do so, or by three or more members of a committee or sub-committee of the authority, trust or body they constitute. The same members will be asked to consider reports renewing the authority for detention under section 20. Health Authorities and Trusts can also discharge a patient maintained under contract in a mental nursing home. The managers should be prepared to review the question of discharge patients and their relatives (who also have the power to discharge under section 23 (see para 102) are still dissatisfied after discussions with the responsible medical officer. Where a hearing is necessary it should be arranged with as little delay as possible.

Authorised officers

58   Regulation 3(6) permits the delegation to individual officers or to a

class of officers the function of making records or reports under the Act. Regulation 4(2) similarly permits the delegation of functions relating to the rectification of admission documents. The authorisation of officers to perform the functions covered by regulations 3(6) and 4(2) should be by a resolution of the appropriate body. It will probably be convenient to authorise all officers holding certain types of posts.

Delivery of documents

59 Regulation 3 provides that any document, other than an application for admission, which is to be delivered to the managers, may either be sent by post or delivered personally to the managers or to any person authorised by them to receive documents on their behalf. These documents include; a report under section 5 which authorises the detention of a patient not previously liable to be detained; a report by the responsible medical officer which renews the authority for detention under section 20; and an order for the discharge of a patient, or a notice of intention to make such an order given by the nearest relative under section 23 or 25; and the written record of the nurse's holding power under section 5. These documents will often either be delivered by hand, or signed on the hospital premises, and an application for admission must be delivered by hand; in any case documents do not take effect until delivered to the person authorised to receive them. The only exception to this is where the nurse has exercised his holding power (see para 28 and 29.) Some of the documents, particularly reports under section 5 and emergency applications under section 4, may need to be received outside normal office hours. A patient's relative may wish to hand a notice of intention to discharge the patient to a nurse or social worker when visiting the hospital. The managers should ensure that suitable officers or classes of officers are authorised to receive documents, bearing these circumstances in mind.

The responsible medical officer

60 The definition of responsible medical officer is covered in 5(c) above. The responsible medical officer has certain powers and duties under Parts II and III of the Act including the power to grant leave of absence (see para 67); of discharge (see para 102); to make a report preventing discharge by the nearest relative (see para 102); to make a report which renews the authority for detention (see para 96), to report to the Home Secretary in the case of a restricted patient (see para 185) and to make an

application for after-care under supervision (see paras 115-117). All hospital patients should be under the care of a consultant who is in charge in the sense that he is not responsible or answerable for the patient's treatment to any other doctor. It is this doctor who will normally exercise the functions of the responsible medical officer. The examinations and reports authorising renewal under section 20 can be made at any time during a two month period, and these should normally be undertaken by the patient's usual doctor. But there are other functions under the Act requiring swift action (eg the decision whether to issue a report barring discharge by the nearest relative under section 25) and the patient's usual doctor may not be available (eg owing to sickness or absence on annual leave). In that case the doctor who is for the time being in charge of the patient's treatment should exercise the functions of the responsible medical officer. This doctor should normally be another consultant or specialist registrar approved under section 12(2) of the Act.

61   In the case of a restricted patient the responsible medical officer must examine and report to the Secretary of State on the patient including such details as the Secretary of State may require.

The nearest relative (sections 26-30)

62   Various functions are conferred on the patient's nearest relative in connection with applications for admission and discharge, applications for after-care under supervision and applications to a Mental Health Review Tribunal. It is open to the nearest relative to authorise in writing some other person under regulation 14 to perform his functions under the Act. The authorised person does not have to be related to the patient. Such authorisation may be given at any time, whether a question of admission to hospital or guardianship has already arisen or not, and it may be revoked at any time. It lapses on the death of the person who made it. While in force it confers the functions of the nearest relative on the person authorised to the exclusion of the person initially defined as nearest relative. The functions of the nearest relative may also be removed from the nearest relative as defined and conferred on some other person by a county court (sections 29 and 30, see paras 107-112).

63   The nearest relative is defined in section 26. If a patient has two relatives of equal standing (for example, father and mother), the elder

takes precedence. If the patient ordinarily resides with, or cared for by one or more relatives, or persons acting as such, they will take precedence over others. The definition of husband or wife includes a person with whom the patient has been living with as a husband or wife for not less than 6 months although such a person does not take precedence over a legal spouse unless there has been a separation or desertion. A person of either sex who has resided with the patient for 5 years or more is also counted as a relative, although he or she comes last in the list. However, as this person becomes a relative residing with the patient (see above), he will, in most circumstances, become the patient's nearest relative.

Reclassification of the patient's disorder

64   Section 16 provides for the reclassification of a patient who is detained for treatment under section 3 or is subject to guardianship under section 7. If it appears to the appropriate medical officer (responsible medical officer or nominated medical attendant) that a patient is suffering from a different form of mental disorder from the one or more forms specified on the application he may report that to the hospital managers or guardian on form 22 or 23. The report may name an additional form of disorder which exists together with the other or it can replace the previously recorded form with another. The original application then has effect as if the new form of mental disorder were recorded on it. The nearest relative and the patient must be informed of the reclassification and either of them may then apply to a Mental Health Review Tribunal within 28 days (section 66).

65   A case requiring reclassification could arise, for example, where a patient with an underlying psychopathic disorder was admitted for the treatment of an episode of mental illness. If the treatment of the mental illness were successful, but the psychopathic disorder remained, the responsible medical officer might want to reclassify the disorder from mental illness to psychopathic disorder. If so, he would have to consider whether further treatment in hospital was likely to alleviate or prevent a deterioration of the patient's psychopathic disorder (and whether the other conditions for detention were still satisfied).

66   Section 16(2) ensures that a patient who is reclassified as suffering from psychopathic disorder or mental impairment (but not from mental

illness or severe mental impairment) does not continue to be detained in hospital unless the disorder is treatable. In these cases the responsible medical officer must include in his report a statement of his opinion as to whether continued medical treatment in hospital is likely to alleviate or prevent a deterioration in the patient's condition .

Leave of absence from hospital

67   Section 17(1) provides that the responsible medical officer may grant a patient leave to be absent from the hospital in which he is liable to be detained, subject to any conditions the responsible medical officer thinks necessary in the interests of the patient, or for the protection of other people. Leave of absence can be given either for a temporary absence, or on a specific occasion, after which the patient is expected to return to hospital, or as a period of trial of the patient's suitability for discharge. Leave can be extended in the absence of the patient (section 17(2)). The responsible medical officer may not grant leave if the patient is remanded to hospital under section 35 or 36 or detained under a section 38 interim hospital order.

68   Section 17(3) states that the responsible medical officer may direct that the patient must remain in custody during his leave if it is necessary in the interests of the patient or for the protection of other persons. The patient may be kept in the custody of an officer on the staff of the hospital or of any other person authorised in writing by the managers of the hospital. These kinds of arrangement would allow detained patients to have escorted leave for outings, to attend other hospitals for treatment, or to have home visits on compassionate grounds. If a patient is granted leave of absence on condition that he stays in another hospital, he may be kept in the custody of any officer on the staff of the other hospital.

Recall from leave

69   If a patient is on leave and it appears to the responsible medical officer that it is necessary to recall the patient to hospital in the interests of the patient's health or safety or for the protection of other persons he may do so by giving notice to the patient or the person in charge of the patient during his leave (section 17(4)). Such a recall can only be made if, in the opinion of the responsible medical officer, the patient's condition makes it necessary for him to become an in-patient (R v Hallstrom, ex p.

W.; R v Gardner, ex p. L (1986) 2 All ER 306). A patient cannot be recalled if the period of his detention has lapsed (section 17(5)). A restricted patient can be recalled by the Home Secretary at any time until the restriction order is lifted.

Absence without leave

70 Section 18 provides powers for retaking patients who are absent without leave from hospital, or from the place where they are required to live (by the conditions of their leave or by their guardian), or who fail to return from leave either at the end of leave or when recalled. A patient who is liable to be detained in a hospital may be retaken by any approved social worker, any officer on the staff of the hospital where he is liable to be detained (but see para 71), any person authorised in writing by the managers of the hospital where the patient is liable to be detained, or any police officer (see paras 313-317). A patient who is absent without leave while under guardianship may be taken into custody by any officer on the staff of a local social services authority, any police officer, or any person authorised in writing by the guardian or a local social services authority (section 18(3)).

71 Section 18(2) provides for the return of patients who go missing while on leave of absence. If such a patient is, as a condition of his leave, required to reside in a hospital other than the one in which he is formally liable to be detained, he may be taken into custody by a member of staff of the hospital where he is on leave, or anyone authorised by the managers of that hospital.

Time limits for retaking patients absent without leave

72 Section 18(4), as amended by the Mental Health (Patients in the Community Act) 1995, sets out the new time limits for retaking patients absent without leave. Patients may be returned for up to six months after going absent, or until the expiry date of the current authority for their detention or guardianship, whichever is later. If at the time the person goes absent the authority for detention or guardianship has been renewed in accordance with section 20, but the new period has yet to begin, the renewal is ignored and the six month limit for returning the patient applies.

73   These time limits do not apply to patients subject to restrictions under section 41 or 49 of the Act who continue to be liable to be returned at any time. They also do not apply to patients who are imprisoned and released from prison while still liable to detention under the Act. Under section 22 such ex-prisoners may be returned to hospital within 28 days of their release from prison.

74   If a patient remains absent without leave after the period set out in paragraph 72 above has expired he cannot be retaken and a fresh application for treatment or guardianship would have to be made if compulsory powers were still appropriate. Section 18(5) states that a patient cannot be taken into custody under section 18 if the period of his detention under one of the following short-term powers has expired: admission for assessment (section 2(4)), emergency admission (section 4(4)), the detention of an in-patient by his doctor (section 5(2)) or by a nurse (section 5(4)).

Powers for retaking patients in any part of the UK, Channel Islands or Isle of Man

75   Section 88 permits patients who are absent without leave from hospitals (but not from the place where they are required to live by a guardian) in England and Wales to be retaken in any other part of the United Kingdom, the Channel Islands or the Isle of Man. Patients can be retaken in these places by anyone who has power to retake them in England and Wales under section 18 or by the equivalent to approved social workers in Scotland or Northern Ireland (see section 88(3)) or by the police of the country where they are found.

Special provisions as to patients absent without leave

76   If a patient who has absconded returns to the hospital or place where he is required to be not more than 28 days after absconding, or is taken into custody during that period, section 21A enables the patient's appropriate medical officer to renew the detention or guardianship under section 20 without further formality. If the authority for detention or guardianship has expired during his absence, or has less than seven days to run on his return section 21 extends it for up to a week from the date of his return.

77   If the patient returns later than 28 days after absconding, the patient's appropriate medical officer must comply with the provisions of section 21B if the detention or guardianship is to be renewed. Section 21B states that the appropriate medical officer must examine the patient within a week of his return. Again if the authority for detention or guardianship has expired, or has less than seven days to run, section 21 extends it by up to one week from the date of the patient's return. The medical officer must decide in the light of his examination of the patient, whether the conditions for continuing liability to detention or guardianship are met and, if they are, must make a report to the hospital managers or local social services authority. Form 31A or 31B should be used in every case[2]. The effect of such a report is explained below. In the case of patients who are liable to be detained (but not those subject to guardianship) the appropriate medical officer must consult an approved social worker, and another professional concerned with the patient's medical treatment, before making a report. The patient must be informed that the report has been made. If a report is not made the liability to detention or guardianship will end (even if the original expiry date has not been reached).

78   If the report under section 21B is made before the date when the original authority would have expired its effect is to restore that authority, which then runs until the original expiry date. However if the original authority has less than two months to run the medical officer may specify that the report should also have the effect of a renewal report under section 20. The authority for detention and guardianship is then renewed for the appropriate period (6 or 12 months) prescribed by section 20(2).

79   If the report under section 21B is made after the date when the original authority would have expired it automatically has the effect of a section 20 renewal report. The new authority (whether for 6 or 12 months) then runs from the expiry date of the old one.

80   The report under section 21B may specify a different form of mental disorder to that which appeared in the original application. The appropriate medical officer does not then need to submit a separate reclassification report under section 16 of the Act.

---

2 Including where the patient's liability for detention or guardianship has a maximum of
   7 days to run contrary to what was said in EL(97)26.

Transfer of patients detained in hospital

81 The hospital in which the patient is liable to be detained is named in the application for admission. Section 19(3) allows a patient to be detained in any other hospital administered by the same managers. Section 123(1) permits the Secretary of State to direct a patient's transfer from one high security hospital to another, and section 123(2) permits him to direct the transfer of a high security hospital patient to a hospital which is not a high security hospital.

82 Detained patients moving from one hospital to another which is not under the same managers should be formally transferred under section 19 using the procedure laid down in regulation 7, unless he or she can be discharged and can continue as an informal patient (see HSG(96)28). The formal authority for transfer (form 24) should not be signed until the arrangements for the transfer have been finalised. The authority for transfer is given by the managers of the transferring hospital (regulation 7). The managers and where relevant, Special Health Authorities, will probably wish to give a general authority to senior staff to authorise transfers. The authority to detain, and the power of discharge, are transferred to the managers and the responsible medical officer at the new hospital from the date on which the patient is admitted. The authority to transfer is valid for 28 days (see regulation 9). Detention documents must be transferred to the receiving hospital with the authority for transfer (see para 93). In the case of patients detained in mental nursing homes, the patient may be transferred to another mental nursing home under the same managers without a formal procedure, but a note of the transfer should be kept with the admission documents (regulation 7(4)). Any transfer of a restricted patient between hospitals, even where the hospitals are administered by the same Trust, is subject to the prior agreement of the Home Secretary.

Transfer from hospital to guardianship

83 A patient may be transferred to guardianship under the procedure laid down in regulation 7. The responsible local social services authority should be consulted, their agreement obtained and recorded (in part II of form 25), and the necessary arrangements made before the authority for transfer (form 25) is sent to them. Where the guardian is a private person, his agreement must also be obtained and recorded in part III of form

25. The transfer takes effect on the date specified by the local social services authority when they confirm the arrangements for the transfer. Until that date the patient remains liable to be detained but there is no reason why, if he is not already on leave, he should not be given leave under section 17 to take up residence outside the hospital before the date. Transfers may be authorised in respect of patients detained under either section 2 or 3. The authority for transfer is valid for 14 days (see regulation 9).

Need to consult nearest relative about patient's transfer

84 The patient's nearest relative should normally be consulted before a patient is transferred to another hospital or to guardianship, and he should be notified when the transfer has taken place. His consent to the transfer is not a statutory requirement, but he has the power of discharge (see para 102-105).

Transfer of patients under guardianship

85 Transfer from one guardian to another can take place under section 10, or, depending on the circumstances, under section 19. In the latter case the procedure laid down in regulation 8 must be followed. If a guardian wishes to give up guardianship he can arrange this by giving notice to the responsible local social services authority (section 10(1)). Under section 10 the guardianship passes automatically to the authority if the guardian dies. Guardianship could subsequently be transferred to another individual under regulation 8 if this were desirable.

86 When guardianship is to be transferred to an individual guardian who has already come forward or to a local social services authority in another area, the procedure under regulation 8 applies. The authority for transfer should be given by the existing guardian on form 26. This authority is then subject to confirmation by the responsible local social services authority (to be recorded in part II of form 26), and takes effect from the date specified by them. Where the guardian is a private person, his agreement must also be obtained and recorded in part III of form 26. Immediately after the transfer the new guardian (if an individual) must appoint a nominated medical attendant (see para 43), and notify the authority of the nominated medical attendant's name and address and the address at which the patient lives (regulation 12).

Temporary guardians

87   Section 10(2) allows the responsible local social services authority, or any person authorised by them, to act temporarily on behalf of a guardian who is ill or incapacitated. The authority or person acting as guardian under this sub-section acts as an agent for the real guardian and may not go against any wishes or instructions he may express.

Unsatisfactory guardians

88   If the responsible local social services authority considers that they should receive the patient into guardianship because the present guardian is unsatisfactory on the grounds mentioned in section 10(3), an application can be made to the county court for an order under that sub-section, even if the present guardian is unwilling to give up guardianship.

Admissions to hospital of patients under guardianship

89   If a patient under guardianship requires treatment in hospital and there is no need to detain him there, he may be admitted informally. He then remains under guardianship unless discharged from guardianship or transferred. Guardianship can also remain in force if the patient is admitted to hospital on an application for admission for assessment under sections 2 or 4. It does not remain in force if the patient is admitted for treatment under section 3 (section 6(4)).

Compulsory admission to hospital for treatment of patients under guardianship

90   If it is decided that the patient needs to be detained in hospital for more than 28 days, an application for admission for treatment may be made under section 3, or he may be transferred under regulation 8(3). In either of these cases guardianship lapses as soon as the application for admission or the authority for transfer takes effect. The procedure for transfer is similar to the procedure for admission under section 3, and the application does not take effect until it is accepted by the managers of the hospital to which it is addressed. The responsible local social services authority must take such steps as are practicable to inform the nearest relative of the transfer and consult him in the same way as for an admission under section 3 (see para 30 and regulation 8(3)). A county court

order under section 29 conferring the functions of the nearest relative on some other person does not expire when a patient is transferred under regulations but it does expire if for any other reason the patient ceases to be liable to detention or subject to guardianship.

Applications for transfer to hospital from guardianship

91   A transfer to hospital is subject to the conditions set out in regulation 8(3) and must be authorised by the responsible local social services authority on form 27 and accompanied by an application for admission for treatment (form 9) and two supporting medical recommendations (form 28 or 29). The provisions of section 12 apply to the medical recommendations. The provisions of section 13 (duty of the approved social worker) and section 11(4) (consultation with nearest relative) apply to the application for admission for treatment. The approved social worker concerned has a duty to consult the nearest relative under section 11(4). The provisions of section 15 concerning the rectification of applications and recommendations do not apply to recommendations given in support of a transfer. The application and recommendations should be scrutinised carefully to make sure they comply with the requirements of the Act and regulations before the authority for transfer is signed.

92   A correctly completed authority for transfer to hospital, together with an application for admission for treatment, is sufficient authority to take the patient to hospital and detain him there, as long as he is admitted within 14 days beginning with the date of the later of the two medical examinations on which the recommendations are based (see regulation 9). On the transfer of the patient the managers of the hospital must record his admission on form 14. Guardianship ceases on the date of admission and the patient is then in the same position as any other patient admitted under section 3. In particular he has the same right to apply to a Mental Health Review Tribunal (this is the effect of section 19(2)(d)).

Documents

93   When a patient is transferred under section 10 or 19, the documents authorising guardianship or detention, including the authority for transfer, should be sent to the hospital or guardian to which the patient is transferred. The former hospital or guardian should retain copies of these documents.

Expiry or renewal of authority for detention or guardianship

94   Section 20 contains the provisions governing the duration of the authority for the detention for treatment, or guardianship, and its expiry and renewal.

95   The initial authority for detention or guardianship lasts for 6 months, as does the first renewal. Subsequent renewals are for one year. This means that the responsible medical officer must review the need for continued detention or guardianship after four months and ten months and then every year. Any patient except one subject to a hospital order (see paras 244-245) has the right to apply to a Mental Health Review Tribunal within the first six months, and again in the second six months if his detention or guardianship is renewed. Subsequent applications may be made once in every 12 month period of detention.

96   Section 20(3) requires the responsible medical officer to examine a patient detained for treatment during the two months preceding the day on which the authority for his detention is due to expire. The patient can only be recalled to hospital from the community to undergo this examination if the patient's responsible medical officer is also satisfied that the patient needs a period of in-patient treatment at that hospital. It is therefore unlawful to recall a patient to hospital when the intention is merely to facilitate the renewal of the patient's detention under section 20 (R v Hallstrom ex p. W, R v Gardner, ex p. L (1986) 2 All ER 306). If it appears to the responsible medical officer that the patient should continue to be detained the responsible medical officer should report that to the hospital managers using form 30 and this report should be kept with the admission documents. Before he makes a report, the responsible medical officer must satisfy himself that all the conditions set out in section 20(4) are satisfied. These conditions, which must be satisfied for the renewal of the authority to detain, are substantially the same as the conditions for admission for treatment, but in the case of a mentally ill or severely mentally impaired patient there is an alternative to one of the conditions. The date of renewal is the date when the authority to detain was due to expire and not the date of the responsible medical officer's report.

Conditions for the renewal of detention

97 The first of the conditions for renewal of detention is that the patient is suffering from mental illness, severe mental impairment, psychopathic disorder or mental impairment and that the disorder is of a nature or degree which makes it appropriate for him to receive medical treatment in a hospital. This is the same condition as in section 3(2)(a) and it ensures that detention can only continue if the patient is still suffering from one of the four named disorders, and if the disorder is serious enough to make hospital treatment appropriate. The second condition is that hospital treatment is likely to alleviate or prevent a deterioration of the patient's condition. (This is the same as section 3(2)(b) but for the purposes of renewal the condition is applied to all four forms of mental disorder.) Alternatively, in the case of a patient suffering from mental illness or severe mental impairment, it is sufficient that the patient, if discharged, is unlikely to be able to care for himself, to obtain the care he needs or to guard himself against serious exploitation. The third condition is that it is necessary for the health or safety of the patient, or for the protection of others that he should receive medical treatment in a hospital, and that it cannot be provided unless he continues to be detained. This is the same as section 3(2)(c). The last part of this condition means that a patient cannot continue to be detained if he is willing and able to receive treatment as an informal patient.

Conditions for the renewal of guardianship

98 Section 20(6) provides for the renewal of the authority for guardianship. It requires the responsible medical officer or nominated medical attendant (see para 43) to examine the patient during the two months before the authority for guardianship expires. If it appears to the doctor that it is necessary in the interests or the welfare of the patient or for the protection of other persons that the patient should remain under guardianship he must report that on form 31 to the local social services authority (or to an officer authorised on their behalf) and to the guardian when he is an individual. Guardianship may only be renewed if the conditions for a guardianship application (see para 39) apply to the renewal as to the original application. The date of renewal is the date when the guardianship is due to expire and not the date of the doctor's report.

Recording a change in the form of mental disorder

99 Section 20(9) provides for cases where the responsible medical officer or nominated medical attendant decides, after examining the patient, that he is suffering from a disorder or form of disorder different from that named on the original application. If a report made under section 20(3) or (6) names a different form of mental disorder from that named in the application, this has the effect of reclassifying the patient and there is no need for a separate report under section 16 (see para 64).

Renewal

100 Sections 20(3) and 20(6) require the hospital managers or local social services authority to inform the patient if they do not discharge him. The managers or local social services authority should consider whether or not to use their powers to discharge the patient (see section 23(3)). Those who are authorised to exercise the power of discharge (see para 57) should therefore consider the renewal report and record their decision at the bottom of form 30 or 31. They should give the patient a hearing unless he or she does not wish to contest the renewal.

101 Normally the whole procedure outlined above should be completed within the two month period allowed for the doctor's examination, and the patient should be informed, by the managers, or local social services authority, of their decision no later than the renewal date. If, however, there is any delay it is the renewal report itself which gives the continued authority for detention whether or not it has been considered by the managers (section 20(8) and R v Managers of Warlingham Park Hospital ex p. B (1994) 22 BMLR 1); and the patient should in any case be informed of the report before the renewal date. The patient's right to apply to a Mental Health Review Tribunal applies from the date of renewal.

Discharge by responsible medical officer, nearest relative or hospital managers

102 In all cases patients admitted for treatment or assessment may be discharged by the responsible medical officer, the nearest relative or the hospital managers. Section 23(4)(5) of the Act enables the hospital managers to delegate their power of discharge to either three or more of their numbers or to three or more members of a committee or sub-committee

that has been specially created for this purpose. The responsible medical officer may discharge the patient without reference to the hospital managers. If the nearest relative wishes to discharge the patient he must give the hospital managers not less than 72 hours notice in writing of his intention. There is no prescribed form of notice but there is a form (34) for the nearest relative to use for the order itself if he wishes. The notice and order for discharge must be served either by delivery of the order or notice at the hospital to an officer of the managers authorised by them to receive it, or by sending it by prepaid post to those managers at that hospital (regulation 3(3)). If the responsible medical officer thinks that, if discharged, the patient is likely to act in a manner dangerous to other persons or himself, the responsible medical officer may within that 72 hours report his view on form 36 to the hospital managers (section 25).

103 The effect of such a report is to prevent the nearest relative from discharging the patient then or at any time in the subsequent six months. If this report is issued in respect of a patient detained for treatment, the managers must inform the nearest relative in writing without delay, and should remind him of his right to apply to a Mental Health Review Tribunal within 28 days (section 66(1)(g) and (2)(d)). In the case of a patient detained for assessment the nearest relative has no right to apply to an Mental Health Review Tribunal if discharge is barred but the patient himself has the right to apply to a Tribunal during the first 14 days of detention, and again if he is subsequently detained for treatment (see para 232).

104 Where a patient is detained in a mental nursing home for assessment or treatment he may be discharged by the Secretary of State, and if the patient is maintained in such a home under contract with a health authority, NHS trust or Special Health Authority he may be discharged by that body (section 23(3)).

105 The nearest relative's written notice of intention to discharge may be delivered in any of the ways described in paragraph 59. The 72 hour period starts to run from the time when the notice is received by an authorised person, or is delivered by post at the hospital to which it is addressed. Therefore all hospitals in which patients are detained should have suitable arrangements for opening post, whether delivered by hand or by the Post Office, at weekends and during holidays. As soon as the

notice is received, the time of receipt should be recorded and the responsible medical officer should be informed.

Discharge from guardianship by responsible medical officer, local social services authority or nearest relative

106 A patient who is subject to guardianship may be discharged by the responsible medical officer, the responsible local social services authority, or the nearest relative. Discharge by the nearest relative cannot be barred, and is effective when the responsible local social services authority receives the order for discharge. The nearest relative may use form 35 to order discharge if he wishes. The power of discharge can be exercised by three or more members of the local social services authority or by three or more members of a committee or sub-committee of the authority.

Appointment by a court of an acting nearest relative

107 Sections 29 and 30 contain various provisions to enable the patient's nearest relative to be displaced and for an acting nearest relative to be appointed. Section 29 gives the county court power to make an order directing that the functions under the Act of the nearest relative shall be exercised by another person, or by a local social services authority. An application for such an order may be made by any relative of the patient, any other person with whom the patient last resided before entering hospital, or by an approved social worker.

108 There are four grounds for making an order under section 29, and they are set out in section 29(3)(a)-(d). Sub-sections (a) and (b) cover circumstances where the patient has no nearest relative as defined in the Act, or where it is not reasonably practicable to identify his nearest relative, or where the nearest relative is too ill or mentally disordered to act as such. In the case where there is no nearest relative there is no obligation to seek an order, but this may be done if someone comes forward who wishes to perform the function of the nearest relative. Section 29(5) provides that an order made on these grounds may specify a period for which the order will remain in force, unless it is discharged. One example of a way in which a court might use this power would be to specify that the order should cease on the date when the eldest child of the patient reached 18, so that he could then take on the role of nearest relative. Sub-sections (c) and (d) relate to cases where the nearest relative has been

acting unreasonably in objecting to an application for admission for treatment or for guardianship, or in attempting to discharge the patient from detention or guardianship. In these cases it will be for the approved social worker who wishes to make the application, in consultation with his superiors, and with the doctors who are prepared to give medical recommendations, to consider whether he should apply for a county court order.

Discharging or varying the court order about the nearest relative

109 Section 30 gives the court power to discharge or vary an order under section 29, and also specifies the duration of an order which has not been discharged. Section 30(4) means that the order lasts either for the period specified under section 29(5) or until the patient is discharged from detention or guardianship if he was detained in hospital for treatment or subject to guardianship at the time the order was made or became so within the following three months. However, the order does not lapse in the event of a transfer between hospital and guardianship, or between hospitals or guardians.

110 An application to a county court on the grounds specified in section 29(3)(c) or (d) (see para 108) that the nearest relative is likely to discharge the patient unreasonably cannot be used to prevent a patient's discharge on the order of the nearest relative but see R v Wilson, exp. Williamson [1996] C.O.D. 42. A responsible medical officer's report barring discharge should be used for this purpose (see para 102). However, a county court order can be used to prevent the power of discharge being used unreasonably a second time. In such cases the staff of the hospital concerned should consult the local social services authority, and if it is decided to apply to a county court, the hospital should provide any necessary evidence to support the application. An application should only be made if it is expected that the patient will be re-admitted within 3 months of the order being made under section 66. A displaced relative may apply for the patient's discharge to a Mental Health Review Tribunal during each 12 month period of detention.

111 An application to the county court may be made while the patient is detained for assessment, or he can be admitted for assessment while an application to the court is pending. In such cases the patient may be de-

tained under section 2 until the county court proceedings are disposed of, including the time for lodging an appeal (which is 21 days after the making of the court's order), and if an appeal is lodged, the time taken to determine it. Once an order is made the patient can be detained for a further 7 days.

112 Where jurisdiction under sections 10, 29 and 30 of the Act is exercised by the county court, the county court rules, which are made by the County Court Rule Committee, will govern the proceedings.

Part IIA

After-care under supervision (Supervised Discharge)

The purpose of after-care under supervision

113 After-care under supervision is an arrangement by which a patient who has been detained in hospital for treatment under the provisions of the Act may be subject to formal supervision after he is discharged. Its purpose is to help ensure that the patient receives the after-care services to be provided under section 117 of the Act (see para 275). It is available for patients suffering from any form of mental disorder but is primarily intended for those with severe mental illness.

Statutory responsibilities

114 The Mental Health (After-Care under Supervision) Regulations 1996 allow for most of the Health Authority's statutory functions relating to after-care under supervision to be delegated to a body with whom the health authority has contracted to provide section 17 services. Such a body is referred to throughout this Memorandum as the provider unit. This would in most cases be a NHS trust, but could be an independent or voluntary sector provider. Where in relation to any patient a health authority has delegated such functions to a provider unit, a local social services authority with after-care under supervision functions in relation to those patients, it may delegate most of them to the same provider unit.

Applying for after-care under supervision (section 25A)

115 An application for after-care under supervision (a supervision application) may be made only by the patient's responsible medical officer at a time when the patient is liable to be detained under the Act. The responsible medical officer should consider making an application if he is satisfied:

- that the patient is suffering from one of the four categories of mental disorder defined in section l(2) of the Act: and
- that there would be a substantial risk of serious harm to the health or safety of the patient or safety of other people, or of the patient being seriously exploited, if the patient did not receive after-care services under section 117 of the Act; and
- that supervision is likely to help ensure that the patient receives those services.

All three of these conditions must be met.

The responsible medical officer must also be satisfied:

- that the patient is 16 years of age or over;
- that he is currently liable to be detained under section 3, 37, 47 or 48 of the Act (this includes patients who have been granted leave of absence under section 17); and
- that he is an unrestricted patient, that is not subject to restrictions under section 41 or 49 (conditional discharge under section 42 of the Act is available for restricted patients). An application may however be made if the patient was formerly subject to restrictions which have been lifted or expired.

116 A patient must be liable to be detained in hospital at the time when the application is made. After-care under supervision takes effect when the patient leaves hospital or, in the case of a patient on section 17 leave, at the point when he is discharged from liability to detention. If for any reason a patient remains in hospital on an informal basis after ceasing to be liable to be detained, the supervision application may still take effect when he eventually leaves provided this is within six months of the application being accepted.

117 A supervision application may he made in respect of a patient who is subject to a Community Care Order under the Mental Health (Scotland) Act 1984 - the equivalent provision to after-care under supervision in Scotland - and who wishes to live in England or Wales. This is governed by a separate procedure which is explained (with the corresponding arrangements for patients wishing to move from England to Scotland) in paras 132 and 133.

Consultation (section 25B)

118 The responsible medical officer is responsible for ensuring that both the current and proposed future care team are consulted about the arrangements to be made for the patient's care after discharge from hospital, and about any requirements to be imposed (see para 126-127) and that agreement about the care plan is reached by all involved. The Act specifies certain people who must be consulted about the making of the supervision application. These are:

- the patient
- one or more members of the team caring for the patient in hospital
- one or more members of the team who will be caring for the patient in the community
- the person, if anyone, who will be acting as an informal carer: that is someone whom the responsible medical officer believes will play a substantial part in the care of the patient in the community but will not be professionally concerned in the provision of services
- the patient's nearest relative unless there is no practicable way in which he can be contacted. A patient may however object to consultation with the nearest relative, unless he will also be acting as the patient's informal carer. The responsible medical officer may then consult the nearest relative only if the patient is known to have a propensity to violent or dangerous behaviour towards others and the responsible medical officer thinks such consultation appropriate.

119 The Act stipulates that the local social services authority which has the duty to provide after-care services under section 117 must be consulted by the Health Authority about the application after it has been made. But since the application must be accompanied by a statement of the after-care services which will be provided it follows that the local social services authority's agreement to the care plan and the supervision arrangements will in fact need to be secured before the application is made.

Submitting the supervision application (section 25B)

120 The application for after-care under supervision should be made on form 1S. The application must include the names of the supervisor and

the community responsible medical officer (these roles are explained in para 128) as well as those of the nearest relative (if any) and of any informal carer who has been consulted about the application. The application will normally be submitted to the provider unit which is responsible for the health component of the after-care services (see para 124). The provider unit needs to identify an individual officer who will be responsible for handling the documentation.

Supporting documentation (sections 25B and 25C)

121 The application must be supported by the written recommendation of an approved social worker (using form 3S) and another doctor (using form 2S). The Act requires that the latter should if possible be a doctor who will be professionally concerned with the patient's medical treatment in the community. This should normally be the community responsible medical officer (see para 128) unless the patient's responsible medical officer will also be acting in that role. In the latter case it is preferable for the recommendation to be given by the patient's general practitioner. If the responsible medical officer is unable to identify another doctor who will be involved in the patient's treatment after he leaves hospital the recommendation may be made by any other doctor, including a member of the staff. Either of the recommending professionals could also be the patient's supervisor. Both the doctor and the approved social worker are given powers under the Act to inspect records relating to the patient's detention or treatment in hospital, or to the provision of after-care services for the patient under section 117. If the supporting recommendation or the application itself is found to be incorrect or defective it may be amended within 14 days of being accepted by the Health Authority if the Health Authority consents.

122 A written recommendation in support of the supervision application may not be made by:

- the responsible medical officer or a close relative of the responsible medical officer;
- anyone who receives or has an interest in the receipt of any payments made on account of the maintenance of the patient;
- a close relative of the patient or of the other professional supporting the recommendation.

'Close relative' for these purposes is defined as husband, wife, father, father-in-law, mother, mother-in-law, son, son-in-law, daughter, daughter-in-law, brother, brother-in-law, sister, or sister-in-law (see section 25D(10)).

123 A supervision application must also be accompanied by:

- written confirmation from the community responsible medical officer and the supervisor that they are willing to act in those capacities (this is included in form 1S);

- a statement of the after-care services to be provided (as in the care plan);

- details of any requirements to be imposed on the patient (see paras 126-127).

Accepting the supervision application (sections 25A and 25C)

124 After-care under supervision can only come into effect after the application is accepted. Before accepting the application, the Health Authority (or provider unit) must consult the local social services authority named in the application to confirm that those elements of the after-care services for which it will be responsible have been agreed. The provider unit should inform the patient's supervisor, community responsible medical officer and general practitioner of the acceptance of the application. After-care under supervision cannot take effect until the patient is discharged from hospital. But, for the purposes of determining when supervision would expire (unless renewed), it will be deemed to have effect from the date the application was accepted (see section 25G(1)).

Informing the patient (section 25B)

125 The responsible medical officer must inform the patient (both orally and in writing) and anyone else who has been consulted that an application is being made; what after-care services it is proposed will be provided; any requirements to be imposed on the patient (see para 126-127); and the names of the community responsible medical officer and supervisor. The Health Authority (or provider unit) must inform the patient (orally and in writing) that the supervision application has been accepted and the implications of this for the patient. In particular the patient's right to

apply to a Mental Health Review Tribunal must be explained. The local social services authority and anyone else who has been consulted must be told when the application is accepted. Copies of the written information given to the patient should also be sent to the patient's nearest relative (if this person has been consulted) and any informal carer.

Requirements (section 25D)

126 The health authority (or provider unit) and the local social services authority can jointly impose any of the following requirements on a patient who is subject to after-care under supervision:

- that the patient should live in a particular place;
- that the patient should attend a particular place at set times for medical treatment, occupation, education or training;
- that the supervisor, a doctor, an approved social worker or a person authorised by the supervisor should be allowed access to the patient at his place of residence.

127 A requirement to attend for medical treatment does not carry with it any power to impose medication or other treatment against the patient's wishes. The Act gives the supervisor (or a person authorised in writing by the supervisor) the power to take and convey a patient to a place where he is required to reside or to attend for medical treatment, occupation, education or training. It follows that the power is available only where the after-care under supervision arrangements include such requirements.

Medical officers and supervisors

128 The Act gives specific responsibilities to designated individual members of the care team, namely the supervisor and the community responsible medical officer:

- The supervisor is responsible for monitoring the after-care under supervision arrangements and for liaising with other members of the community team and for co-ordinating their work where necessary. He should ensure that the team reviews the patient's after-care plan well before the date when it falls to be renewed, and whenever any shortfall in the arrangements is identified (see paras 129-130). The supervisor has powers to require entry to the patient's place of residence and to convey the patient to a place where he is required to live or attend (see para 127).

- The community responsible medical officer is responsible for the patient's treatment in the community. He must be a registered medical practitioner approved by the Secretary of State under section 12(2) of the Act as having special experience in the diagnosis or treatment of mental disorder (see para 55). The community responsible medical officer has powers (set out in para 128) to renew and terminate after-care under supervision, and to reclassify the patient's mental disorder, in each case after taking into account views expressed during consultation with a range of people.

Review and modification of after-care under supervision (section 25E)

129 If the supervisor, community responsible medical officer or care team consider that any part of the care plan, or any requirement placed upon the patient, needs to be changed they must (on behalf of the Health Authority and the local social services authority who are responsible for section 117 after-care) consult the following people about the proposed modifications:

- the patient;
- any informal carer;
- the patient's nearest relative, where practicable and unless the patient objects, subject to what is said in paragraph 118

and take their views into account. Neither the supervisor, community responsible medical officer nor the provider unit can change the after-care under supervision in the care plan unless authorised by the Health Authority and the local social services authority.

130 If changes are made the patient and any person consulted should be informed. The patient must be told both orally and in writing, and should be given a copy of the revised care plan and requirements. The patient's nearest relative (if consulted) must be told in writing about the modifications. Those concerned must be informed in the same way if there is a change of community responsible medical officer or supervisor for any reason - including where the patient has moved from one area to another (see para 131). If the patient refuses to receive an after-care service or to

comply with a requirement the supervisor or care team can consider whether they should recommend to the patient's community responsible medical officer that the supervision should end (see para 138), or whether they should inform an approved social worker that, in their view, he should be admitted to hospital for treatment under section 3 of the Act (for the effect of a section 3 admission on the after-care under supervision, see para 138).

Patients moving within England and Wales

131 If the patient wishes to move to an area in England or Wales covered by a different health and local social services authority, the supervisor will need to take the lead, before the patient moves, in contacting the professionals who will be responsible for section 117 after-care services in the new home area. There will need to be direct contact between the present community responsible medical officer and his counterpart in the new area. It will be for the health and local social services authority in the new area to decide whether to continue the after-care under supervision arrangements. If so the arrangements set out in paragraphs 118 and 125 for consulting and informing the patient and others about modifications to the care plan will apply.

Patients moving to or from Scotland (section 25J)

132 A supervision application may be made for a patient who is subject to a community care order (the Scottish equivalent of after-care under supervision) under the Mental Health (Scotland) Act 1984 and who wishes to move to England or Wales. In these cases the application will be made by the prospective community responsible medical officer in England or Wales. The details are set out in the Mental Health (Patients in the Community) (Transfers from Scotland) Regulations 1996. The applicant will be responsible for consulting members of the care team in Scotland, the person (if anyone) who will be acting as the patient's informal carer and the nearest relative (subject to what is said in para 118) as well as members of the prospective care team. It will be essential before making the application to ensure that both the Health Authority and the local social services authority agree to provide section 117 after-care for the patient. In practice the initiative is likely to be taken by the care team in Scotland and the application should, if possible, be supported by recommendations from the patient's special medical officer (the equivalent in Scotland

of the community responsible medical officer) and the patient's after-care officer in Scotland. If (exceptionally) a recommendation cannot be obtained from either the special medical officer or the after-care officer it may be given by, respectively, another doctor or an approved social worker. Once the application is accepted and the patient has moved the arrangements are as for anyone else subject to after-care under supervision in England and Wales.

133 There are similar arrangements under section 35K of the 1984 Act for patients subject to after-care under supervision wishing to move from England or Wales to Scotland. In that event the special medical officer in Scotland will be required to consult the English or Welsh care team, any informal carer and the patient's nearest relative (subject to what is said in para 118) about the proposed community care order.

Reclassification of a patient (section 25F)

134 The community responsible medical officer may submit a reclassification report, using form 4S, to the Health Authority (or the provider unit), stating that the patient is suffering from a mental disorder other than that shown on the supervision application, provided that he has ensured that at least one other person concerned with the patient's medical treatment (unless there is none) has been consulted. The supervision application will then be treated as if the revised classification had been specified in the first place. The patient must be informed both orally and in writing and his nearest relative must be informed in writing (if practicable and unless the patient objects).The patient has the right to apply to a Mental Health Review Tribunal against the reclassification, as does his nearest relative, within 28 days of the reclassification report being furnished.

Renewal of after-care under supervision (section 25G)

135 After-care under supervision will apply initially for a maximum period of six months, and can thereafter be renewed for a further six months and then for periods of a year at a time. The community responsible medical officer must examine the patient in the two months preceding the expiry date. The community responsible medical officer must also ensure that the following are consulted and their views taken into account:

- the patient;
- the supervisor;
- one or more persons (unless there is none) professionally concerned with the patient's medical treatment in the community;
- at least one member of the patient's care team;
- any informal carer;
- the patient's nearest relative (if practicable and unless the patient objects, subject to what is said in para 118).

136 If after-care under supervision is to be renewed, the community responsible medical officer must submit a renewal report (using form 5S) to the Health Authority (or provider unit) stating:

- that the patient is suffering from one of the four categories of mental disorder defined in section 1(2) of the Act; and
- that there is still a substantial risk of serious harm to the health or safety of the patient or to the safety of other people, or of the patient being seriously exploited, unless the after-care is supervised; and
- that supervision will help to ensure that the patient continues to receive the section 117 services.

137 The Act requires the renewal report to be submitted to the responsible health and local social services authorities. However, if both the health and local social services authorities have delegated their functions to the provider unit or another body (see para 114) the community responsible medical officer will need to submit the report only to that body. The body receiving the report must ensure that the following people are informed:

- the patient, orally and in writing. The implications of renewal for the patient must be made clear. In particular, the right to apply to a Mental Health Review Tribunal must be explained;
- any informal carer;
- the nearest relative, in writing (if practicable and unless the patient objects, subject to what is said in para 118)

that after-care under supervision has been renewed.

Ending of after-care under supervision (section 25H)

138 The community responsible medical officer may at any time direct that the patient should cease to be subject to after-care under supervision. Before doing so, he must ensure that the people who would have had to be consulted if a renewal application were being made (see para 135) are consulted and must take their views into account. The community responsible medical officer should make the direction on form 6S to the Health Authority (or provider unit). The Health Authority (or provider unit) must inform the local social services authority that after-care under supervision has been terminated and should note on the form that this has been done. After-care under supervision will automatically be ended if a patient is readmitted to hospital for treatment (under section 3 of the Act) or is received into guardianship. It also ends when a patient has been detained in prison or remanded in custody for more than six months, beginning on the date of the relevant court order. When a patient ceases to be subject to after-care under supervision the same people must be informed as if the supervision were being renewed (see para 138).

Suspension of after-care under supervision (section 25I)

139 When a patient is imprisoned or remanded in custody for six months or less or is detained in hospital under section 2 of the Act the arrangements for providing after-care services under after-care under supervision will be suspended. On the patient's release or discharge, after-care under supervision will be reactivated and continue for the remainder of the original period if any. If after-care under supervision would have lapsed whilst the patient was detained in custody or in hospital, it will be deemed to have been extended for 28 days after his release or discharge. Any renewal (and associated examination) must be made during this period.

140 An emergency admission under section 4 of the Act, or admission to a hospital as a "place of safety" under section 135 or 136, will not end after-care under supervision unless the patient is then detained under section 3 for treatment. If a patient subject to after-care under supervision is admitted to hospital on an informal basis, the arrangements for providing after-care services under supervision should be put into suspense and reactivated when the patient leaves hospital unless the period of after-care under supervision ends while the patient is in hospital.

Powers of the Courts and Home Secretary

Introduction

141 Part III deals with the circumstances in which patients may be admitted to and detained in hospital or received into guardianship on the order of a court, or may be transferred to hospital from prison on the direction of the Home Secretary. In addition to the powers of the courts to make hospital or guardianship orders (section 37), the Act gives the courts four extra powers: remands to hospital for a medical report; remands to hospital for treatment; interim hospital orders; and hospital and limitation directions (sections 35, 36, 38 and 45A). Appendix 7 lists sentencing options for the courts.

Remand to hospital for report on mental condition

142 Section 35 empowers the courts to order the remand to hospital of an accused person for the preparation of a report on his mental condition. This provides an alternative to remanding the accused person in custody for a medical report, in circumstances where it would not be practicable to obtain the report if he were remanded on bail (for instance because he might decide to break a condition of bail that he should reside at a hospital, and the hospital would then be unable to prevent him from discharging himself).

143 The power applies to the following categories of person:

a.   where the power is being exercised by the Crown Court, to any person who is awaiting trial before that court for an offence punishable with imprisonment or who is at any stage of such a trial prior to sentence (other than a person convicted of murder);

b. where the power is being exercised by the magistrates' court, to any person

   i. convicted of an offence punishable on summary conviction with imprisonment; or

   ii. charged with such an offence, if the court is satisfied that he did the act or made the omission charged or if he has consented to the exercise of the power.

144 The power may be exercised only if:

a. the court is satisfied on the written or oral evidence of a registered medical practitioner, approved by the Secretary of State under section 12, that there is reason to suspect that the accused person is suffering from mental illness, psychopathic disorder, severe mental impairment or mental impairment; and

b. the court is of the opinion that it would be impracticable for a report on his mental condition to be made if he were remanded on bail; and

c. the court is satisfied, on the written or oral evidence of the registered medical practitioner who would be responsible for making the report or some other person representing the managers of the hospital, that the patient will be admitted to hospital within seven days of the date of remand.

145 Remand is in the first instance for up to 28 days, after which the accused person may be further remanded for periods of up to 28 days, but only:

a. if it appears to the court, on the written or oral evidence of the registered medical practitioner responsible for making the report, that this is necessary for completing the assessment; and

b. up to a maximum total period of 12 weeks.

146 The power of further remanding the accused person may be exercised by the court in his absence if he is legally represented and his representative is given the opportunity to be heard. The court may terminate

the remand at any time: and the accused person is entitled to obtain a separate medical report from a registered medical practitioner of his own choice, and at his own expense, and to apply to the court on the basis of it for his remand to be terminated.

147 The effect of the remand is, first, to direct a constable (or any other person chosen by the court) to convey the accused person to the hospital specified in the order, and, second, to entrust responsibility for his detention and reappearance in court to the managers of the hospital. The managers may not grant the accused person leave of absence nor may they transfer him to another hospital: if necessary, an application may be made to the court. If the accused person absconds, he may be arrested without warrant by any constable and is then to be brought before the court that remanded him, which may decide on some alternative approach to his case.

Remand to hospital for treatment

148 Section 36 empowers the Crown Court to order the remand to hospital of an accused person for treatment. This provides an alternative to the Home Secretary's power under section 48 to transfer unsentenced prisoners to hospital in an emergency.

149 The power applies to a person who is in custody awaiting trial before the court for an offence punishable with imprisonment (other than murder) or who is in custody at any stage of such a trial prior to sentence.

150 The power may be exercised only if the court is satisfied:

a.   on the written or oral evidence of two registered medical practitioners, one of whom must be approved by the Secretary of State under section 12, that the accused is suffering from mental illness or severe mental impairment of a nature or degree which makes it appropriate for him to be detained in a hospital for medical treatment; and

b.   on the written or oral evidence of the registered medical practitioner who would be in charge of the accused person's treatment, or of some other person representing the managers of the hospital, that the patient will be admitted to hospital within seven days of the date of remand.

151 Paragraphs 145 and 146 above also apply to remands to hospital for treatment under section 36, with the difference that since the purpose of the remand is the accused person's treatment rather than the preparation of a report on him, further remands depend simply on written or oral evidence from the responsible medical officer that a further remand is warranted (but the patient can still apply for the remand to be terminated on the basis of a medical report he has obtained himself).

Interim hospital orders

152 To assist the courts and the hospitals in determining whether it is appropriate to make a hospital order or a hospital direction in respect of an offender, section 38 empowers the courts to make an interim hospital order so that the offender's response in hospital can be evaluated without any irrevocable commitment on either side to this method of dealing with the offender if it should prove unsuitable.

153 The power applies to the same categories of person as do hospital orders (see para 157) but a magistrates' court cannot make an interim hospital order in respect of an unconvicted person.

154 The power may be exercised only if the court is satisfied, on the written or oral evidence of two registered medical practitioners, one of whom must be approved by the Secretary of State under section 12, and one of whom must be employed by the hospital to be specified in the order:

- a. that the offender is suffering from mental illness, psychopathic disorder, severe mental impairment or mental impairment; and

- b. that there is reason to suppose that the mental disorder is such that it may be appropriate for a hospital order to be made in his case; and

- ii. the court is satisfied, on the written or oral evidence of the registered medical practitioner who would be in charge of the offender's treatment, or of some other person representing the managers of the hospital, that the offender will be admitted within 28 days of the order.

155 An interim hospital order may be made in the first instance for a period of up to 12 weeks, and may be renewed for further periods of up to 28 days to a maximum total period of 12 months. Both the power of renewal, and the power to convert an interim hospital order into a hospital order, may be exercised by the court in the absence of the offender if he is legally represented and his representative is given the opportunity to be heard. The court may also terminate the interim hospital order after considering the written or oral evidence of the responsible medical officer and deal with the offender in some other way.

156 The effect of an interim hospital order is first to direct a constable (or any other person chosen by the court) to convey the offender to the hospital specified in the order, and, second, to entrust responsibility for his detention and reappearance in court to the managers of the hospital. The managers may not grant the accused person leave of absence nor may they transfer him to another hospital: if necessary, an application may be made to the court. If the offender absconds, he may be arrested without warrant by any constable and is then to be brought before the court that made the order, which may decide on an alternative way of dealing with him.

Hospital and guardianship orders

157 Section 37 empowers courts to make a hospital or guardianship order in respect of certain categories of offender:

a. where the power is being exercised by the Crown Court, in respect of any person convicted before that court for an offence punishable with imprisonment (other than murder);

b. where the power is being exercised by the magistrates' court;

    i. in respect of any person convicted by that court of an offence punishable on summary conviction with imprisonment; and

    ii. in respect of any person charged before that court with such an offence who would, if convicted, be liable to be made subject to a hospital or guardianship order as a person suffering from mental illness or severe mental impairment, if the court is satisfied that he did the act or made the omission charged.

158 The power to make a hospital order may be exercised if:

a. the court is satisfied, on the written or oral evidence of two registered medical practitioners (one of whom must be approved by the Secretary of State under section 12):

    i. that the offender is suffering from mental illness, psychopathic disorder, severe mental impairment or mental impairment; and

    ii. that the offender's mental disorder is of a nature or degree which makes it appropriate for him to be detained in a hospital for medical treatment; and

    iii. that in the case of an offender suffering from psychopathic disorder or mental impairment such treatment is likely to alleviate or prevent a deterioration of his condition; and

b. the court is satisfied, on the written or oral evidence of the registered medical practitioner who would be in charge of the offender's treatment, or of some other person representing the managers of the hospital named in the order, that the offender will be admitted to that hospital within 28 days of the date of the order; and

c. the offender is described by each of the medical practitioners whose evidence is taken into account as suffering from the same form, or one of the same forms, of mental disorder; and

d. the court is of the opinion, having regard to all the circumstances including the nature of the offence and the character and antecedents of the offender, and to the other available methods of dealing with him, that a hospital order is the most suitable method of dealing with the case.

159 The power to make a guardianship order may be exercised if:

a. the court is satisfied, on the written or oral evidence of two registered medical practitioners, one of whom must be approved by the Secretary of State under section 12:

    i. that the offender is suffering from mental illness, psychopathic disorder, severe mental impairment or mental impairment; and

    ii. in the case of an offender who has attained the age of 16 years, the mental disorder is of a nature or degree which warrants his reception into guardianship; and

b. the court is of the opinion, having regard to all the circumstances including the nature of the offence and the character and antecedents of the offender, and to the other available methods of dealing with him that a guardianship order is the most suitable method of dealing with the case.

160 Where a patient is admitted to hospital under a hospital order or placed under guardianship by a guardianship order, any previous application for admission or guardianship and any previous hospital or guardianship order still in existence ceases to have effect unless a restriction order is in place at the time. However, if the later order is subsequently quashed on appeal the previous application or order remains in effect and will validate any period of detention under the later order unless that period lasted for 6 months or more.

161 The court may not, at the same time as making a hospital or guardianship order in respect of an offender, pass a sentence of imprisonment or impose a custodial sentence on a young offender or impose a fine or make a probation order or a supervision order or an order for the offender's parent or guardian to enter into a recognizance to take proper care of and exercise proper control over him; but the court may otherwise make any other order which it has the power to do.

Restriction orders

162 Section 41 empowers the Crown Court (but not magistrates' court) when making a hospital order, to make in addition a restriction order. Orders restricting a discharge may be made under section 41 only when a hospital order is also made, not when a guardianship order is made.

163 The requirements for the making of a restriction order are:

a. that it appears to the court, having regard to:
    i. the nature of the offence, and
    ii. the antecedents of the offender, and
    iii. the risk of his committing further offences if discharged, that a restriction order is necessary for the protection of the public from serious harm; and

b. that at least one of the registered medical practitioners whose evidence is taken into account has given oral evidence to the court.

164 Any restriction order may be either for a specified period or without limit of time and may be terminated at any time by the Home Secretary under section 42(1). On the making of a restriction order the court has the power to specify that the patient be admitted to a particular unit of the hospital in question (see section 47 of the Crime (Sentences) Act 1997). Where a hospital unit is specified, any power to detain the patient in hospital relates to his detention in that unit. In particular, the Home Secretary's powers under section 41 of the Act to control leave, transfer or discharge from hospital (see para 183) will apply to leave, transfer or discharge from that unit.

Committal to the Crown Court for a restriction order

165 A magistrates' court has no power to make a restriction order. If such a court is satisfied that the conditions exist in which it could make a hospital order, but also feels that a restriction order should be made in addition, it may commit an offender (if over 14 years old) to the Crown Court, under section 43 of the Act. Section 44 provides that the magistrate may direct his detention, pending the hearing of the case by the Crown Court, in any hospital to which arrangements have been made to admit him. This will normally be the hospital which had already agreed to admit the patient in the event of the magistrates' court itself making a hospital order.

166 A patient admitted to hospital under section 44 is to be detained as if he were subject to a hospital order with a restriction order (see paras 182-187) and is to be produced from the hospital to attend the Crown Court. It will be the managers' duty to arrange for his attendance with an appropriate escort. It will not be necessary to obtain the Home Secretary's consent to leave of absence from the hospital for this purpose. If a considerable time elapses between the hearing by the magistrates and the hearing by the Crown Court, the hospital authorities should arrange for two fresh medical reports to be submitted to the court (one by a doctor approved under section 12). They should also arrange for at least one doctor to be available to give oral evidence. After appearing before the

Crown Court the patient will not be liable to be taken back to the hospital compulsorily unless that court makes a hospital order.

167 If while the patient is detained under section 44 his mental condition deteriorates to such an extent that he is unlikely to be fit to appear before the Crown Court on the day of the hearing, the court should be notified immediately. In those circumstances the court may either adjourn the case or, if the patient is suffering from mental illness or severe mental impairment, it may make a hospital order, with or without a restriction order, in his absence under powers conferred by section 51. The court can make a hospital order in the patient's absence only if it is satisfied, on the written or oral evidence of at least two doctors, that the patient is suffering from mental illness or severe mental impairment of a nature or degree which makes it appropriate for the patient to be detained in hospital for medical treatment. In informing the court of a patient's unfitness to appear, the hospital authorities should enquire whether it is likely to wish to proceed in the patient's absence, and if so they should arrange for two doctors, one of whom must be a doctor approved under section 12 of the Act, to attend at the court to give evidence of the patient's mental state.

Power to make hospital and limitation directions

168 Section 45A of the Act empowers the Crown Court, when imposing a prison sentence on offenders convicted of an offence other than murder, to give a direction for their immediate detention in a specified hospital (a "hospital direction"), together with a direction that they be subject to the special restrictions in section 41 of the Act (a "limitation direction"). A hospital and limitation direction may be given if the court is satisfied on the evidence of two doctors that :

(i)   the offender is suffering from a psychopathic disorder; and

(ii) the disorder is of a nature or degree which makes it appropriate for him to be detained in hospital for medical treatment; and

(iii) such treatment is likely to alleviate or prevent a deterioration of his condition.

169 Before it makes a hospital and limitation direction the court must:

(i) have considered making a hospital order (except where a mandatory life sentence must be imposed under section 2 of the Crime (Sentences) Act 1997), and

(ii) be satisfied on the written or oral evidence of the doctor who would be in charge of the offender's treatment, or of some other person representing the managers of the hospital named in the direction, that arrangements have been made for the admission of the offender to that hospital within 28 days of the direction.

170 On the making of a hospital and limitation direction, the court has the power to specify that the offender be admitted to a particular unit of the hospital in question.

Medical evidence

171 Courts may make a hospital order or guardianship order or include in a probation order a requirement under section 3 to undergo treatment of the Powers of Criminal Courts Act 1973, on the basis of written medical reports, but they may, if they wish, call the doctors to give oral evidence. If a court proposes to make either a restriction order in addition to a hospital order or a hospital and limitation direction it is required to hear oral evidence from at least one doctor. Medical reports should normally be submitted in writing to the court in advance of the hearing, and the doctors should be prepared to give oral evidence if required. They may be asked to do so at comparatively short notice, especially in the Crown Court.

Place of safety pending admission to hospital

172 If the hospital can admit the patient within 28 days of the court's sitting, but not immediately, the court may make a hospital order and also make an order under section 37(4) or 43A(5) for the patient to be detained in a place of safety while waiting admission to the hospital. 'Place of safety' is defined to include any hospital the managers of which are willing to receive the patient. In such a case, the doctor seeking a bed should, if possible, secure an undertaking from another hospital (eg a hospital with beds set aside for emergency cases) to accept the patient for the interim period. If there is difficulty in obtaining a bed, the doctor may need to seek the help of the Health Authority. Section 45A(5) gives the Crown Court a similar power to direct that an offender be taken to and

detained in a place of safety pending his admission to hospital under a hospital and limitation direction.

Courts' power to request Health Authorities for information about hospital places

173 Section 39 places a duty on health authorities to respond to requests from courts for information about hospitals which could admit a person in respect of whom the court is considering making a hospital order, or hospital and limitation direction. The court will not be obliged to go through the Health Authority if a placement can be arranged directly. If one of the doctors examining the patient is on the staff of the hospital to which admission might be desirable there should be no need for such a request. There may sometimes be doubt as to the patient's normal place of residence or as to other factors which affect the appropriate hospital for admission and in this case it will fall to the Health Authority to advise the court. A court requesting information should get in touch with the Regional Mental Health Lead at the respective Regional Office of the NHS Executive for details of the relevant Health Authority contact.

Community care - need to consult social services authorities

174 If the reporting doctors wish to recommend community care from the local social services authority with or without guardianship, they should consult the local social services authority for the offender's home area. It will be for the local social services authority to inform the court whether it is prepared to provide community care, including, if necessary, itself acting as guardian; if a private guardian is proposed it will be for the local social services authority to inform the court that it has approved the proposed guardian and to send a statement signed by him that he is willing to act.

175 Under 39A a court may request the appropriate local social services authority to inform it whether the authority or another person approved by the authority is willing to receive the offender into guardianship and, how the powers conferred by the guardianship could be used. The authority must comply with such a request by the court.

Detention in a place of safety

176 If an order is made for a patient's detention in hospital as a place of safety under section 37(4) while awaiting admission to the hospital named in the hospital order, he may be detained there for not more than 28 days. There are no provisions for discharge or leave of absence. If the patient escapes, section 138 allows him to be retaken by the person who had his custody immediately before his escape or by a constable or by any member of staff of, or person authorised in writing by the managers of the hospital named in the hospital order. If the hospital order was not accompanied by a restriction order, he may not be retaken after the time limits described in section 18(4) (see para 72). If the hospital order was accompanied by a restriction order, he may be retaken without limit of time. Section 50(4) provides in effect that time ceases to run while patients are at large; or they remain liable to recapture indefinitely. If he is retaken, the time during which he was absent does not count towards the 28 days for which he may be detained in the place of safety.

177 Where it proves impossible to admit the patient to the hospital specified in the order within the 28 day period, the hospital managers should refer the case back to the sentencing court in good time so that a further order can be made to allow a further 28 day period in which a bed may become available. The Secretary of State (or the Secretary of State for Wales) may give directions for the patient's admission to some other hospital if an emergency or some other special reason prevents admission to the hospital named in the hospital order.

Rights of appeal against conviction and sentence

178 All patients admitted to hospital on a hospital order will have certain rights of appeal either to the Court of Appeal (Criminal Division) or to the Crown Court. A leaflet describing the rights of appeal and the appeal procedure is available for the hospitals concerned (leaflet 12), so that they can advise any patient who wishes to appeal of the procedure to be followed. If a patient appeals from the decision of a magistrates' court to the Crown Court he must be present in court when his appeal is heard. On the day of the hearing, of which the hospital managers will be notified by the Crown Court, he should be taken to the court with an escort.

If the patient appeals to the Court of Appeal, he will not necessarily have to appear before the court, but if the court orders him to be present he should similarly be taken with an escort. If any patient who is required to appear before the court is, in the opinion of the responsible medical officer, unfit to appear, the Crown Court or the Registrar of Criminal Appeals, as the case may be, should be notified immediately. If on appeal the patient's conviction is quashed or another sentence is substituted for the hospital order the authority for his detention in hospital lapses automatically (but see para 160).

Effect of a hospital order without restrictions or of a guardianship order

179 The effect of a hospital order is, first, to confer authority on a constable, an approved social worker or any other person directed by the court to convey the patient to the hospital specified in the order within 28 days and, second, to confer authority on the managers of the hospital to admit the patient within that period and to detain him.

180 The effect of a guardianship order is to confer on the authority or person named in the order the same powers as a guardianship application made and accepted under Part II of the Act.

181 A patient admitted to hospital under a hospital order without restrictions or placed under guardianship by a guardianship order is treated essentially the same as a patient admitted to hospital or placed under guardianship under Part II of the Act. The necessary modifications to the provisions of Part II are made in Part I of Schedule 1 to the Act. A major difference between a Part III patient and one admitted under Part II is that the power of the patient's nearest relative to discharge him from hospital or guardianship under section 23(2) does not apply to Part III patients. A further difference is that a patient admitted under a hospital order does not have the right to apply to a Mental Health Review Tribunal until six months after the date of the making of the order, if the order is renewed.

Effect of a hospital order with a restriction order

182 When a patient is admitted to hospital on a hospital order accompanied by a restriction order he is subject to the special restrictions and

modifications set out in sections 41 and 42 of the Act.

183 The patient may not be given leave of absence or be transferred to another hospital (even if managed by the same hospital managers) or to guardianship or be discharged except with the Home Secretary's consent, although a restricted patient can also apply to be discharged by a Mental Health Review Tribunal (see para 244). Requests for consent to leave of absence, transfer or discharge should be sent to the Home Office by the responsible medical officer or the managers. When consent to transfer is given, the document in which consent is given should be attached to the authority for transfer (form 24) and sent with it to the receiving hospital, a copy being kept by the hospital which the patient is leaving.

184 The authority for detention does not expire while the restriction order is in force. It does not, for instance, expire if a patient absents himself without leave and is not returned to hospital within the periods mentioned in section 18; the patient may be returned to the hospital under that section at any time so long as the restriction order is in force. Similarly, the limit on leave of absence, at the end of which the authority for detention expires under section 17, does not apply. The provisions for expiry and renewal under section 20 also do not apply; nor do the provisions for reclassification under section 16.

185 It is, however, the duty of the responsible medical officer to keep continually under review the suitability for discharge of all patients who are subject to restriction on discharge, as of all other patients, and under section 41(6) he is obliged to report at least annually to the Home Secretary on each restricted patient in his care. The initiative in seeking the Home Secretary's consent to discharge lies with the responsible medical officer and the managers, and they should not hesitate to seek consent when they consider the patient's condition warrants it. The Home Secretary may sometimes think it necessary, in view of his special responsibility for the protection of the public, to refuse or postpone his consent to discharge, but he will rely on the hospital authorities to bring cases to his notice. Hospital managers should not assume that consent to discharge will not be given before the end of the period named in a restriction order made for a limited time, since the Home Secretary has discretion to consent to discharge at any time.

186 In addition to his power to consent to discharge by the responsible medical officer or by the managers, the Home Secretary is given power under section 42(2) to discharge patients subject to restriction orders himself. If the Home Secretary (or a Tribunal) discharges a patient the discharge may be conditional or absolute. A patient who is conditionally discharged may be recalled to hospital by the Home Secretary at any time during the currency of the restriction order. The conditions which the Home Secretary would normally think it appropriate to attach to a conditional discharge are that the patient should live in a particular household and be under the supervision of a psychiatrist and a responsible person (usually a probation officer or social worker) who would undertake to submit reports to the Home Secretary on the patient's progress from time to time and to inform the Home Secretary and the responsible medical officer if the patient's mental condition appeared to be deteriorating.

187 A restriction order ceases to have effect at the end of any period named in the order by the court or may be brought to an end at any time on the direction of the Home Secretary under section 42(1). When this happens, section 41(5) provides that the patient is to be treated as though he had been admitted to hospital in pursuance of a hospital order without a restriction order made on the date on which the restriction order ceased to have effect.

Effect of hospital and limitation direction

188 A hospital and limitation direction authorises a constable or any other person directed to do so by the court to convey the patient to the hospital specified in the hospital direction within a period of 28 days. If within this period it appears to the Secretary of State that by reason of an emergency or other special circumstance, it is not practicable for the patient to be taken to the hospital specified in the hospital direction, he may give directions for the patient's admission to some other hospital. The hospital managers of the relevant hospital are authorised to detain him there subject to the provisions of the Act.

189 A hospital direction has the same legal effect as a transfer direction made under section 47 of the Act, and a limitation direction has the same legal effect as a restriction direction made under section 49 of the Act.

The effect of these sections is explained in paragraphs 195-199. Under section 45B of the Act the patient's responsible medical officer is required to report at least annually to the Home Office on a patient detained under a hospital direction and limitation direction.

Notification of hospital orders and hospital directions to the Home Office

190 When a patient is admitted to hospital under a hospital order, the hospital is asked to send to the Home Office a copy of each order. This applies both to hospital orders made together with a restriction order and to those made without, but not to interim hospital orders, place of safety orders, remands to hospital or patients admitted by direction of the Home Secretary. However, if a patient originally admitted to hospital in one of the latter ways subsequently becomes subject to a hospital order, the hospital should notify the Home Office as if the patient were a new admission. The hospital should also notify the Home Office of hospital and limitation directions. The address to which copies of hospital orders should be sent is:

Home Office
Research and Statistics Directorate
Offenders and Corrections Unit
Room 262
Queen Anne's Gate
London
SW1H 9AT

Transfer to hospital of prisoners

191 Sections 47 to 53 make provisions for the transfer on the direction of the Home Secretary from prisons, remand centres and such institutions to hospitals of people suffering from mental disorder. Different considerations apply to sentenced prisoners from those which apply to other prisoners because of the need ultimately to bring the latter before a court or to resolve in some other way the proceedings in which they are involved. There are further distinctions between different categories of unsentenced prisoners. Sections 47, 49 and 50 apply to sentenced prisoners: sections 48, 49 and 51-53 apply to the various categories of other prisoners.

Sentenced prisoners

192 The power to transfer sentenced prisoners applies to any person serving a sentence of imprisonment or other form of detention specified in section 47(5).

193 The power may be exercised only if:

a. the Home Secretary is satisfied, by reports from at least two registered medical practitioners, one of whom must be approved under section 12:

i. that the prisoner is suffering from mental illness, psychopathic disorder, severe mental impairment or mental impairment; and

ii. that the mental disorder is of a nature or degree which makes it appropriate for the prisoner to be detained in a hospital for medical treatment; and

iii. in the case of a prisoner suffering from psychopathic disorder or mental impairment, that such treatment is likely to alleviate or prevent a deterioration of his condition; and

b. both medical reports describe the prisoner as suffering from the same form or one of the same forms of disorder; and

c. the Home Secretary is of the opinion, having regard to the public interest and all the circumstances, that it is expedient to direct the prisoner's transfer.

194 If transfer to a hospital is recommended, the Health Authority for the patient's home area will be sent copies of the medical reports and will be asked to say which hospital can admit the patient. In the case of a prisoner suffering from mental illness, this will be done by the prison medical officer at the same time as he sends the report to the Home Office; the Health Authority should notify both the Home Office and the prison which hospital will take the patient. In the case of prisoners suffering from other forms of mental disorder, the approach to the Health Authority will be made by the Home Office itself after preliminary consideration of the reports; the notification of the vacancy should be sent to the Home Office. On being informed that a vacancy is available, the Home Office will if satisfied that it is right to do so issue a transfer direction - ie a warrant directing the patient's transfer.

Sentenced prisoners - transfer directions with or without restriction directions

195 A transfer direction made under section 47 has the same effect as a hospital order made by a court without an order restricting discharge (see paras 179-181). The direction is valid for 14 days, after which a fresh direction will be necessary if the patient has not been admitted to the hospital or mental nursing home.

196 When giving a transfer direction in respect of a sentenced prisoner, the Home Secretary has discretion also to give a restriction direction under section 49. This direction has the same effect as a restriction order made by the court (see paras 182-187). When he makes a restriction direction the Home Secretary can specify that the patient be admitted to a particular unit of the hospital in question.

197 A restriction direction ceases to have effect on the earliest date the person would have been released from prison if he had not been transferred from hospital (section 50(3)). Hospitals will be notified at the time of transfer of the date on which restrictions will expire. But if a patient has been absent without leave before that date the period of absence does not count towards the period of sentence. If any such patient is absent without leave for more than 24 hours, the hospital should inform the Home Office of the absence and when he returns to the hospital. The Home Office will then advise the hospital of the effect on the period of restriction.

198 Where both a transfer direction and a restriction direction are in force, the Home Secretary may direct the patient's return to prison (or other penal institution) or discharge him from the hospital on the same terms on which he could be released from prison. Before he can return a patient to prison the Home Secretary must first be notified by the responsible medical officer or any other registered medical practitioner or a Mental Health Review Tribunal that the patient no longer requires treatment in hospital for mental disorder or that no effective treatment for his disorder can be given in the hospital to which he has been transferred. The responsible medical officer should notify the Home Office at once in writing if he considers that a patient meets these criteria. If the Home Secretary decides that the patient should be returned to a prison or other

institution he will issue a warrant directing the patient's removal from the hospital under section 50 of the Act.

199 The restriction on discharge on any patient transferred under section 47 may be terminated at any time by the Home Secretary. When this is done, or when the period of restriction indicated in the transfer direction expires, the position of the patient and his nearest relative will be as described in para 181. The patient may also be discharged from hospital with the consent of the Home Secretary and in certain circumstances by a Mental Health Review Tribunal (see para 253).

Other prisoners

200 The power to transfer prisoners other than those covered by section 47 applies to

a. all other persons detained in a prison or remand centre, including

b. persons remanded in custody by a magistrates' court, and

c. civil prisoners other than those covered by section 47, and

d. persons detained under the Immigration Act 1971.

201 The power may be exercised only if the Home Secretary is satisfied by reports similar to those required under section 47 that:

a. the prisoner is suffering from mental illness or severe mental impairment; *and*

b. the mental illness or severe mental impairment is of a nature or degree which makes it appropriate for the prisoner to be detained in hospital for medical treatment; *and*

c. the prisoner is in urgent need of such treatment.

202 As with transfer directions given under section 47, both reports must describe the prisoner as suffering from the same form or at least one of the same forms of mental disorder, and the direction is valid for 14 days. The effect of the direction is the same (see para 195). When giving a transfer direction in respect of a prisoner in categories a. and b. of paragraph 200 the Home Secretary *must* also give a restriction direction, and

when giving a transfer direction in respect of a prisoner in categories c. and d. he may give a restriction direction.

203 The consequences of a transfer direction given in respect of a prisoner in category a. of para 200 are as follows. The transfer direction will cease to have effect when the patient's case has been fully dealt with by the appropriate court. Alternatively, if meanwhile the Home Secretary is notified by the responsible medical officer, any other registered medical practitioner or a Mental Health Review Tribunal that:

i.   the patient no longer requires treatment in hospital for mental disorder; or
ii. no effective treatment for his disorder can be given in the hospital to which he has been transferred,

the Home Secretary *may* direct the patient's return to prison (or other penal institution).

204 Another alternative is that the court may order the patient to be returned to prison or released on bail if it is satisfied on the written or oral evidence of the responsible medical officer as to either of the conditions in i, or ii above. Finally, if:

a.   it appears to the court that it is impracticable or inappropriate to bring the patient before it; and
b.   the court is satisfied, on the written or oral evidence of at least two registered medical practitioners, that the patient is suffering from mental illness or severe mental impairment of a nature or degree which makes it appropriate for the patient to be detained in a hospital for medical treatment,

the court may make a hospital order (with or without a restriction order) in the patient's absence and, in the case of a person awaiting trial, without convicting him.

205 The consequences of a transfer direction given in respect of a prisoner in category b. of para 200 are as follows. The transfer direction will cease to have effect on the expiration of the period of remand to which

the prisoner was subject unless he is then committed in custody to the Crown Court. The prisoner may be further remanded without being brought before the court, but only if he has appeared before the court in the previous six months; and if the prisoner is further remanded in custody the transfer direction will continue in effect. Alternatively, the magistrates' court may terminate the transfer direction if satisfied, on the written or oral evidence of the responsible medical officer, that the patient no longer requires treatment in hospital for mental disorder or that no effective treatment can be given in the hospital to which he has been transferred. The magistrates' court may conduct committal proceedings in the absence of the patient, if satisfied on the written or oral evidence of the responsible medical officer that the patient is unfit to take part in the proceedings and if the patient is legally represented; and if the patient is committed to the Crown Court and the magistrates' court has not terminated the transfer direction on the grounds that the patient no longer requires treatment, etc. the provisions of section 51 (see para 203) will apply.

206 The consequences of a transfer direction given in respect of a prisoner in categories c. or d. of para 200 are as follows. In all cases the direction will cease to have effect on the expiry of the period during which the prisoner would have been liable to be detained. However, in cases where a restriction direction has been given as well as the transfer direction, the Home Secretary may direct the patient's return to prison if he is notified by the responsible medical officer, any other registered medical practitioner or a Mental Health Review Tribunal, that the patient no longer requires treatment in hospital for mental disorder or that no effective treatment for his disorder can be given in the hospital to which he has been transferred.

Detention during Her Majesty's pleasure

207 Section 46 of the Act applies in the comparatively unusual circumstances where a serviceman is found to be not guilty by reason of insanity or unfit to stand trial by a court-martial and ordered to be detained 'during Her Majesty's pleasure', i.e. indefinitely. It gives the Home Secretary power to direct the detention of such a person in hospital (but not in a mental nursing home) as if subject to a hospital order with restrictions.

Criminal Procedure (Insanity) Act 1964

208 Under the Criminal Procedure (Insanity) Act 1964 (as amended by the Criminal Procedure (Insanity and Unfitness to Plead) Act 1991) a defendant before the Crown Court may be found either 'not guilty by reason of insanity' or unfit to plead. In the event of either of these findings the court has the following sentencing options:

(i)   an order (an "admission order") that the accused should be admitted to such hospital as may be specified by the Home Secretary. The court may also direct that the accused is treated as though subject to a restriction order made without limit of time or for a specified period. A direction that the accused be treated as though subject to a restriction order without limit of time must always be made where the offence charged is murder;

(ii)   a guardianship order made under section 37 of the Act;

(iii)   a supervision and treatment order, requiring the accused to co-operate with supervision by a social worker or a probation officer for a period of not more than two years and with treatment (for all or part of that period) by a doctor; or

(iv)   an order for the absolute discharge of the accused.

209 Where a court makes an admission order, the Home Secretary must specify the hospital in which the person will be detained within two calendar months of the date of the order. The court may also give directions for the conveyance to the place of safety and for his detention there pending his admission to the specified hospital within two month period.

210 The Home Secretary will normally, on receiving notification of an admission order from the court, approach the relevant Health Authority explaining the circumstances and asking for a suitable hospital place to be found (or the relevant Special Health Authority where a place in a high security hospital is considered appropriate). This will be a matter of considerable urgency as the statutory period of two months cannot be extended. The Home Secretary is under an inescapable statutory obligation to specify a hospital, and in the last resort is bound to do so even if a hospital's agreement to admit the patient has not first been obtained. The specified hospital is under a legal obligation to admit the patient.

Where the court has directed that a person who has been made the subject of an admission order should be treated as though subject to a restriction order, the Home Secretary has the power to specify that the person be admitted to a particular unit of the specified hospital.

211 Because a patient admitted to hospital under an admission order will not have been tried he may, if he recovers sufficiently, be remitted to prison by warrant of the Home Secretary for this purpose. The general principle observed is that a person who has been accused of an offence ought, if possible, to be brought to trial so that he may have an opportunity of having his guilt or innocence determined by a court. The Home Secretary will consult the responsible medical officer about such a patient's fitness for trial during the first six months of detention, at the end of which period the patient's case, if he has not already applied, will be referred automatically to a Mental Health Review Tribunal for their consideration (see para 236).

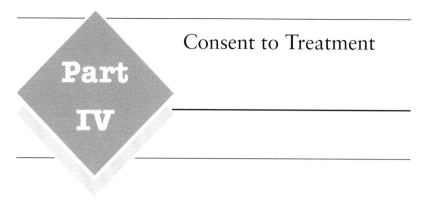

Consent to Treatment

Introduction

212 Part IV (sections 56 - 64) is largely concerned with consent to treatment for mental disorder by detained patients in NHS hospitals and mental nursing homes, but certain safeguards in this part of the Act also apply to informal patients. There are two levels of safeguards. The first level applies to the most serious treatments which require a patient's informed consent *and* an independent second medical opinion (it is these safeguards which apply to informal patients). The second level applies to other serious treatments which require a patient's consent *or* a second opinion. All these safeguards can, however, be set aside where the need for treatment is urgent. The Act itself specifies two treatments to which the different levels of safeguards must be applied - ie psychosurgery which will require a patient's informed consent *and* a second opinion; and drug treatment for more than three months which will require the patient's consent *or* a second opinion. The Act provides for other treatments to be specified in regulations or in the Code of Practice (see paras 216, 220 and 280) which also gives guidance in relation to the medical treatment of mental disorder in general. Any treatment for mental disorder not specified in the Act, regulations or Code of Practice (none has been specified in the Code) may be given without the patient's consent by or under the direction of the responsible medical officer, although an attempt to obtain the patient's consent should be made. Mental Health Act Commission guidance for responsible medical officers on the provisions of the Act governing consent to treatment and on the procedures to be followed when considering treatment are given in circular DDL(84)4. Further relevant information, including form MHAC/1, is contained in the MHAC letter dated September 1984.

Patients to whom Part IV applies

213 Section 56 provides that this part of the Act applies, with certain exceptions, to all detained patients, and extends to informal patients the provisions governing the most serious treatments requiring informed consent and a second opinion. The exceptions are:

a.   patients detained by virtue of an emergency application for assessment but for whom the second medical recommendation has not yet been given or received (section 4);

b.   in-patients detained for 72 hours on a report by their doctor (section 5(2)) or for up to six hours under the nurse's holding power (section 5(4)); accused persons remanded to hospital for a report on their mental condition (section 35); offenders admitted to hospital as a place of safety under a direction made by the court for a period of up to 28 days following the making of a hospital order (section 37(4)); persons suffering or believed to be suffering from mental disorder removed to a place of safety by a warrant made under section 135 or found in a place to which the public have access and removed to a place of safety under section 136 for up to 72 hours.

c.   a patient who has been conditionally discharged under section 42(2), 73 or 74 and has not been recalled to hospital.

214 Patients in categories (a) to (c) above are in the same position as informal patients with regard to treatment (except that they are not covered by section 57) and the common law applies.

Treatments to which Part IV applies

215 Part IV applies to 'any medical treatment .... for ... mental disorder' (section 63). In B v Croydon Health Authority (1995) 1 All ER 683 the court held that those words include treatment to alleviate the symptoms of the mental disorder as well as treatment to remedy its underlying cause.

Treatment requiring consent *and* a second opinion

216 Only one treatment, psychosurgery, is specified in the Act as a treatment requiring consent and a second opinion (section 57). Other treatments can be specified in regulations or in the Code of Practice. One

treatment is specified in regulation 16 - the surgical implantation of hormones for the purpose of reducing male sexual drive.

217 If it is thought desirable to treat a patient with psychosurgery or any other treatment (or a series of treatments - see para 222), specified for this section, the responsible medical officer[1] should seek the consent of the patient in the normal way. If the patient is not considered to be capable of consent, or he does not consent, he cannot be given the treatment. If the patient consents to the treatment and appears to have understood the responsible medical officer's explanation of the nature, purposes and likely effects of the treatment, the responsible medical officer should contact the Mental Health Act Commission (see para 282-289 and Appendix 1). The Commission will send a medical practitioner appointed by them, who may be a medical member of the Commission, and two other appointed persons who are not doctors to consider the validity of the patient's consent. They must be allowed access to all the patient's records, including medical records and documents relating to his detention (if he is detained), and they must be allowed to interview, or in the case of the doctor examine, the patient in private if they wish (see sections 120, 121 and 129). Directions about giving access to persons appointed by the Mental Health Act Commission are contained in Circular HC(83)19.

218 If the appointed medical practitioner, and the two other appointed persons, agree that the consent is valid they will jointly issue a certificate to the effect that the patient is capable of understanding the nature, purpose and likely effects of the treatment in question and has consented to it (form 37 part 1). This certificate is not a substitute for a standard consent form which should be obtained. The appointed medical practitioner has also to consider whether the treatment is appropriate, and, if he is satisfied as to this, will issue a certificate to the effect that, having regard to the likelihood of the treatment alleviating or preventing a deterioration of the patient's condition, it should be given (form 37 part II).

219 Before he issues this certificate the appointed medical practitioner has an obligation (under section 57(3) of the Act) to consult a nurse, and one other person (not a nurse or doctor, probably a psychologist, social

---

1 In this Part of the Act Responsible Medical Officer means the registered medical practitioner in charge of the patient's treatment.

worker or other therapist), who have been professionally concerned with the patient's treatment. The responsible medical officer will need to provide the appointed medical practitioner with the relevant documents and the names of professionals involved with the case. Arrangements should then be made for the appointed medical practitioner to consult the professionals he wishes to approach. It is a requirement that any certificate issued under this part of the Act must be retained with the patient's records so that they can be inspected at any time by the Commission (see HC(83)19). These two certificates (which together make up form 37) constitute the authority for carrying out the treatment.

Treatment requiring consent *or* a second opinion

220 Section 58 applies to the administration of medicine for mental disorder if three months or more have elapsed since the medicine was first given to the patient during a period of detention, and to any other form of treatment for detained patients that may be specified in regulations. There can only be one three month period for medication for mental disorder for the purposes of section 58 in any continuous period of detention, including such a period during which detention under one section is immediately followed by detention under another section. "Detention" for this purpose does not include detention under section 4, 5(2), 5(4), 35, 135 or 136. Subject to the provisions for urgent treatment under section 62 (see para 227) section 58 applies to any administration of ECT to any such detained patient (see regulation 16).

221 If a patient consents to a treatment which comes under section 58, and which the responsible medical officer has proposed and explained to the patient, the responsible medical officer (or a doctor appointed by the Commission) must certify in writing that the patient is capable of understanding the nature, purpose and likely effect of the treatment and has consented to it. He must use form 38 for this purpose whether or not he has also used a standard consent form. If the patient does not consent to a treatment included under this section, and the responsible medical officer, having considered the alternatives, continues to feel that the patient needs that particular form of treatment, he should contact the Mental Health Act Commission. The Commission will send an appointed medical practitioner to consult with two persons professionally concerned with the patient, one of whom must be a nurse and the other neither a nurse

nor a doctor, as well as the responsible medical officer, and give a second opinion as described above (see para 217). Should the appointed medical practitioner agree that, having regard to the likelihood of the treatment alleviating or preventing a deterioration of the patient's condition, the treatment may be given. He or she will certify this on form 39, also indicating either that the patient is not capable of understanding the nature, purpose and likely effect of the treatment or that the patient has not consented to it.

Plan of treatment

222 Section 59 states that any consent or certificate obtained for the purposes of sections 57 or 58 can relate to a plan of treatment which can involve one or more of the treatments specified under the same section and can include a time scale for the administration of the treatments. If a plan of treatment is being considered, the appointed medical practitioner will consider the whole plan, and accept or reject it as a whole. However, it is hoped that there will be scope for discussion between the responsible medical officer and the appointed doctor about details of the plan, so that a generally sound plan need not be rejected because of a minor disagreement. An outline of the plan of treatment will appear on the certificate, and will, of course, be described in detail in the patient's medical records.

Withdrawing consent

223 Section 60 provides for a patient to withdraw his consent to any treatment which comes under section 57 or 58. If a patient withdraws his consent from any treatment or plan of treatment under these sections, the remainder of the treatment must be considered as a separate treatment for the purposes of those sections. This means that if a patient withdraws his consent to a section 57 treatment it must not be given, or if a plan of treatment is in progress, the treatment must cease immediately unless one of the criteria for urgent treatment described in para 227 is met. If a patient withdraws consent to a treatment or a plan of treatment specified for section 58 the responsible medical officer must contact the Mental Health Act Commission immediately so that the requirements of that section can be complied with. Again, the responsible medical officer must cease administering the treatment unless section 62 applies.

Reporting to the Commission

224 Section 61 provides that where the appointed persons have issued certificates under section 57(2) or 58(3)(b) the responsible medical officer must give a report to the Commission on the treatment and the patient's condition:

a. when he reviews the authority for detention under section 20(3) (see para 96);

b. at any time the Commission requires him to do so.

Circular DDL(84)4 gives further information on Review of Treatment as does the Mental Health Act Commission letter dated September 1984.

225 In the case of a patient subject to a restriction order or direction the report must be made:

a. six months after the date of the order or direction if the treatment was given in that period;

b. if the treatment is given more than six months after the date of the order or direction, the next time the responsible medical officer makes a report under section 41(6) or 49(3) (see paras 185 and 189);

c. at any time the Commission requires him to do so.

Commission's power to order that treatment be discontinued

226 Section 61 taken with section 121(2) also provides that the Commission may at any time give notice to the responsible medical officer that a certificate given under section 57(2) or 58(3)(b) no longer applies to the treatment or the plan of treatment after the date it specifies. After that date the responsible medical officer will again have to go through the procedures set out in paras 216-221 before he can continue treatment, unless the grounds for urgent treatment described in para 227 are met.

Urgent treatment

227 Section 62 describes the circumstances under which certain treatments that would otherwise fall within section 57 or 58 may be given to a patient who does not consent or is not capable of giving consent, without following the procedures set down by those sections. Any treatment

may be given which is immediately necessary to save the patient's life. Treatments for mental disorder will, of course, rarely come into this category. Treatment of physical disorder which is neither a symptom of the patient's disorder nor a cause of it, is not covered by this Act, and the patient can only be treated under common law.

228 In addition to treatments for mental disorder immediately necessary to save life, other treatments that may be given under section 62 are:

i.   a treatment which is not irreversible and is immediately necessary to prevent a serious deterioration of the patient's condition (a treatment is considered to be irreversible if it has unfavourable irreversible physical or psychological consequences);

ii.   a treatment which is not irreversible or hazardous and is immediately necessary to alleviate serious suffering by the patient (a treatment is considered to be hazardous if it entails significant physical hazard);

iii. a treatment which is not irreversible or hazardous, is immediately necessary, and represents the minimum interference necessary, to prevent the patient from behaving violently or being a danger to himself or to others.

229 A course of treatment or a plan of treatment may be continued, pending compliance with section 57 or 58 (for example, where a patient withdraws his consent) provided that the responsible medical officer considers that the discontinuance of the treatment or the plan would cause serious suffering to the patient.

230 When treatment is given under section 62 that would, under normal circumstances fall under section 58, the responsible medical officer should immediately contact the Mental Health Act Commission and request a second opinion if that treatment is to continue.

Mental Health Review Tribunals

Part V

231 Each region in England is covered by a separate Mental Health Review Tribunal (Mental Health Review Tribunal). A separate Tribunal covers the whole of Wales. There are five Tribunal offices, four of which provide the administrative support to the Tribunals in England; the other provides administrative support for the Tribunal in Wales. Their addresses are set out at the end of this memorandum in Appendix 2. Further information is available from the Tribunal offices.

Patients detained under Part II of the Act

Applications by patients or their nearest relatives

232 Patients in hospitals, subject to guardianship or after-care under supervision and their nearest relatives may apply to a Mental Health Review Tribunal on the occasions set out below

	Patient may apply	*Nearest relative may apply*
Detained under section 2	In first 14 days of detention	–
Detained under section 3	In first 6 months of detention	–
Reclassified (section 16)	In first 28 days from being informed of report by RMO	In first 28 days from being informed of report by RMO
Received into guardianship	In first 6 months of guardianship	–

	Patient may apply	*Nearest relative may apply*
Transferred to hospital from guardianship	In first 6 months of detention in hospital	–
Detention or guardianship is renewed	At any time in the period for which detention or guardianship is renewed	
RMO bars relative's discharge (section 25)	–	In first 28 days from being informed of report by RMO
Nearest relative barred from acting as such by Order of County Court (section 29)	–	In first 12 months of Order and subsequently once in each 12 month period for which Order is in force.
Detention or guardianship of patient who has absconded is renewed (section 21B)	At any time in period for which detention or guardianship is renewed	–
Reclassified (section 21B)	In first 28 days of being informed of report	
After-care under supervision application (section 25A)	Within 6 months of application being accepted	Within first 6 months of application being accepted
Reclassified (section 25F)	In first 28 days of being informed of report	In first 28 days of being informed of report
After-care under supervision renewed (section 25G)	At any time during the further period of after-care under supervision	At any time during the further period of after-care under supervision

233 In each case only *one* application can be made in the period specified. This application can be made at any time during the period. An application which is withdrawn before it has been determined does not count for this purpose.

Hospital managers' duty to refer cases to a Tribunal

234 Any Part II patient who has been detained for 6 months under section 3 or after being transferred from guardianship under regulations made under section 19 and who has not applied for a Tribunal or had an application made on his behalf by his nearest relative, or had his case referred by the Secretary of State, must be referred to a Tribunal by the hospital managers.

235 If the authority for detention is renewed, and the patient at that time has not had a Tribunal for three years or more, or, if he is under 16, for one year or more, the hospital managers must refer his case to a Tribunal.

Referral of cases by Secretary of State

236 The Secretary of State has the right to refer a patient to a Tribunal at any time.

Powers of the Tribunal

237 The Mental Health Review Tribunal has a range of options in relation to any patient whose case they consider. They have the power to order discharge or delayed discharge from hospital or guardianship, or may recommend leave of absence or transfer to another hospital. They also have the power to recommend to the patient's responsible medical officer that he makes an application for after-care under supervision in respect of the patient. In the case of an un-restricted patient if their recommendation is not complied with, they may reconvene and reconsider the case afresh (R v Mental Health Review Tribunal for Wales, ex p. Hempstock C.O.D. [1997] 443).

238 The Tribunal *must* discharge a patient detained under section 2 if they are satisfied that he is not then suffering from a mental disorder of a nature or degree which warrants his detention in hospital for assessment (or for assessment followed by medical treatment) for at least a limited

period, or if his detention is not justified in the interests of his health or safety or for the protection of others.

239 The Tribunal *must* discharge any other Part II patient if they are satisfied that he is not then suffering from one of the four categories of mental disorder (see paras 7-12) of a nature or degree which makes hospital treatment appropriate; or if his detention is not justified in the interests of his health or safety or for the protection of others or - when the Tribunal is considering an application when the responsible medical officer has barred the patient's discharge by his nearest relative under section 25 - if the patient, if released, would not be likely to act in a manner dangerous to others or to himself.

240 The Tribunal *may* discharge unrestricted patients in cases where the above criteria are not met (for restricted patients see below). In determining whether or not to do this, section 72(2) directs that they should consider, except for section 2 patients, the likelihood of medical treatment alleviating or preventing a deterioration of the patient's condition and, in the case of mentally ill or severely mentally impaired patients, the likelihood of the patient, if discharged, being able to care for himself, obtain the care he needs, or guard himself against serious exploitation.

241 The Tribunal *must* discharge a patient from guardianship if satisfied that he is not suffering from one of the four categories of mental disorder, or that it is not necessary in the interests of the welfare of the patient or for the protection of others that he should remain under guardianship.

242 The Tribunal has a general discretion to discharge a patient who is subject to after-care under supervision and must discharge the patient if they are satisfied that either the application criteria or the renewal criteria are not complied with.

Patients detained under Part III of the Act

Applications in first 6 months of detention

243 Different considerations apply to Part III patients. Such patients have the right to apply to the Tribunal in the first six months of detention only if they fall into one of the following categories:

a.   patients placed under guardianship order;

b.   patients originally detained subject to a restriction order, who remain in hospital after its expiry as if subject to a hospital order made on the date the restriction order expired;

c.   patients originally detained under the Mental Health (Northern Ireland) Order 1986 and transferred to a hospital in England or Wales under section 82;

d.   patients originally detained under mental health legislation in the Channel Islands or the Isle of Man and transferred to a hospital in England or Wales under that legislation;

e.   patients originally detained under the Mental Health (Scotland) Act 1984 and transferred to a hospital in England or Wales under section 77 of that Act;

f.   patients admitted to hospital under an order made under section 5(1) of the Criminal Procedure (Insanity) Act 1964 as substituted by section 3 of the Criminal Procedure (Insanity and Unfitness to Plead) Act 1991;

g.   patients admitted to hospital under sections 47 or 48;

h.   patients admitted to hospital under an interim hospital order.

In the case of patients in categories a.-f., the six months begins from the date of the order or transfer direction: in the case of patients in category g., from the date of the transfer direction.

Hospital orders

244 Part III patients detained in hospital under a *hospital order* have no right to apply in the first 6 months because their case will have been examined at the outset by a court which must have considered medical evidence from two registered medical practitioners. These patients' first opportunity to apply to the Tribunal therefore arises in the second six months of detention (if detention is renewed in the case of unrestricted patients), and thereafter at annual intervals. These entitlements correspond to the rights accruing on renewal of the authority for detention of Part II patients.

245 The nearest relative of a patient detained in hospital (other than a restricted patient) also has the right to apply to the Tribunal at these

intervals. The nearest relative of a patient placed under a guardianship order may apply at any time within the first 12 months and annually thereafter.

Referral of case by the Home Secretary or hospital managers

246 If a Part III patient has not had a Tribunal for three years, his case must be referred to a Tribunal, by the Home Secretary in the case of restricted patients, and the Hospital Managers in the case of other Part III patients. In addition, restricted patients admitted to hospital under section 5(1) of the Criminal Procedure (Insanity) Act 1964 who do not exercise their right to apply to the Tribunal during the first six months of detention (see para 211), or who withdraw any such application, must have their case referred to the Tribunal by the Home Secretary at the end of that period.

Conditionally discharged patients

247 Conditionally discharged restricted patients may also apply to the Tribunal 12 months after discharge and every 2 years thereafter and if such a patient is recalled to hospital the Home Secretary must refer his case to the Tribunal within one month of his being readmitted to hospital.

Powers of the Tribunal in respect of restricted patients

248 The Tribunal's powers in respect of *non-restricted* Part III patients are the same as for Part II patients (see para 251), but they are different for restricted patients. Under section 73 of the 1983 Act a Tribunal *must* order the *absolute discharge* of a patient subject to a restriction order if they are satisfied:

i.   that he is not suffering from mental illness, psychopathic disorder, severe mental impairment or mental impairment or from any of those forms of disorder of a nature or degree which makes it appropriate for him to be liable to be detained in hospital for medical treatment;

     or

ii.   that it is not necessary for the health or safety of the patient or for the protection of other persons that he should receive such treatment;

and

iii. that it is not appropriate for the patient to remain liable to be recalled to hospital for further treatment.

249 Under the same section the Tribunal must order the *conditional discharge* of a patient subject to a restriction order if it is satisfied that the patient should remain liable to recall, but:

i. that he is not suffering from mental illness, psychopathic disorder, severe mental impairment or mental impairment or from any of those forms of disorder of a nature or degree which makes it appropriate for him to be liable to be detained in a hospital for medical treatment;

or

ii. that it is not necessary for the health or safety of the patient or the protection of other persons that he should receive such treatment.

250 Where a Tribunal decides to order the conditional discharge of a patient it may defer its final direction until the arrangements necessary for that purpose have been made. In practice, this means that the Tribunal will expect the detaining hospital to submit proposals for the patient's after-care for the Tribunal's approval. If the Tribunal uses its power to defer it cannot reconvene to reconsider its original decision that the patient be conditionally discharged (Secretary of State for the Home Department v Oxford Regional Mental Health Review Tribunal [1987] 3 All ER 8). It is unlawful for a Tribunal to defer if the purpose of the deferment is to secure the patient's admission to another hospital (Secretary of State for the Home Department v Mental Health Review Tribunal for the Mersey Regional Health Authority [1986] 3 All ER 233).

251 In the case of non-restricted patients, Tribunals 'shall have regard to' the likelihood of medical treatment alleviating or preventing a deterioration of the patient's condition. There is no equivalent of this provision in relation to restricted patients. The effect of this is that although the Tribunal must discharge if the mental disorder is not of a nature or degree which makes medical treatment appropriate (see para 5(g) for definition of medical treatment) the patient's suitability to the treatment being provided in that hospital forms no part of the statutory criteria which a Tribunal will have to consider before authorising the discharge

of a restricted patient. The fact that a restricted patient's condition is not benefiting from the treatment he is receiving does not automatically entitle him to be discharged.

252 In the case of restricted patients the Tribunal has no discretion to discharge the patient if the statutory criteria for discharge set out in paragraphs 238 and 239 are not fulfilled.

Special provisions in respect of patients subject to a restriction direction

253 Patients subject to a restriction direction (see paras 196-199) or a limitation direction (see para 189) are liable to resume serving their sentence of imprisonment if they no longer require treatment in hospital. Under these circumstances, the Tribunal cannot therefore authorise discharge in the normal way. Instead, it has to notify the Home Secretary if it finds that the patient could otherwise be conditionally or absolutely discharged, and may at the same time recommend that if the patient cannot be conditionally discharged he should continue to be detained in hospital rather than being returned to prison. In the case of a patient who was originally a remand prisoner or other prisoner transferred under section 48, the Home Secretary has no discretion: unless the Tribunal has made a recommendation for the patient's detention in hospital, he must return the patient to prison. In the case of a sentenced prisoner, however, it may be that the Home Secretary is able to agree to his discharge. The Home Secretary has 90 days from the date of notification of the Tribunal's finding in which to give notice that the patient may be discharged: if he does not, the patient must be returned to prison unless the Tribunal has made a recommendation that in those circumstances he should remain in hospital.

General powers and procedures of Tribunals

254 In any non-restricted case before it, the Tribunal has power to reclassify the patient as suffering from a different form of mental disorder. Conversely, even if the application was made under section 16 when the patient is reclassified, the Tribunal may direct discharge or one of the other options specified in the Act (see para 237).

Tribunal Rules

255 The Lord Chancellor has made Rules of Procedure under section 78 - the Mental Health Review Tribunal Rules 1983 (Statutory Instrument 1983 No 942). These impose various duties on the 'responsible authority' - in the case of a patient detained in hospital, the managers, in the case of a patient detained under guardianship, the local social services authority, and in the case of a patient subject to after-care under supervision, the Health Authority which has the duty under section 117 to provide after-care services to the patient.

Application

256 The Tribunal will send the responsible authority a copy of the application, and ask them to submit a statement giving certain information including a medical report by the responsible medical officer (the form of this Statement is set out in the Schedule to the Tribunal Rules). The authority should inform the Tribunal at once if the patient has no right to apply - eg if he is not subject to detention under the Act and is free to discharge himself. In all other cases they should forward their statement as soon as possible, immediately where there is an assessment application and in any case within three weeks. Where the applicant is a restricted patient detained in hospital the Home Secretary will also provide a statement. Where the applicant is a conditionally discharged patient, the Home Secretary will provide the whole statement. The responsible authority or Home Secretary may ask, giving supporting reasons, that part of the statement be withheld from the patient (see Rules 6(4) and 12).

257 The Tribunal has the power under the Rules to obtain any information they think necessary, including the power to subpoena witnesses. The medical member of the Tribunal will in all cases be required to examine the patient or take such other steps as he considers necessary to form an opinion on the patient's mental condition. In addition, any doctor authorised by the patient or applicant to the Tribunal may examine the patient in private and require any records relating to the patient's detention or treatment in hospital to be produced for his inspection.

Legal Aid and Assistance

258 Legal assistance under the Green Form Scheme is available to help patients and other applicants with limited means to obtain advice and assistance from a solicitor. Patients may also be provided with legal representation for the hearing under the Assistance By Way of Representation scheme which is available regardless of means. Both hospital managers and any member of staff, including a social worker, may obtain advice from the Legal Aid Area Offices to assist those detained patients who have no access to solicitors or legal advice. A list of Legal Aid Area Offices in England and Wales and the areas covered by them is at Appendix 3.

259 The responsible authority may be represented by anyone they authorise for this purpose. This will normally be the responsible medical officer who should be ready to answer any questions the Tribunal may have about the patient's suitability for discharge and his home circumstances. Other people, in particular social workers, may be brought in as witnesses when necessary. Legal representation is not usually necessary for the responsible authority.

Part VI

Removal and return of Patients within the United Kingdom

260 Part VI of the Act provides powers under which certain categories of detained patients (not those detained under section 35, 36 or 38), conditionally discharged patients and patients under guardianship may be moved between England and Wales and other parts of the United Kingdom, the Channel Islands and the Isle of Man, while remaining under detention or guardianship or continuing to be conditionally discharged; or may be retaken in those places when absent without leave from hospitals or institutions. It also provides powers for moving mentally disordered patients who are neither British citizens nor Commonwealth citizens with the right of abode here from hospitals in England and Wales to countries abroad. Appendix 5 to this memorandum gives a brief resume of the procedures to be followed and the corresponding provisions in the Scotland and Northern Ireland mental health legislation.

Removal between England and Wales, Scotland, Northern Ireland, the Channel Islands and the Isle of Man

261 If arrangements are made at the request of a patient or his relatives for him to go to another part of the United Kingdom, the Channel Islands or the Isle of Man, and if it is not necessary to keep the authority for detention in operation while he is being moved, he may be discharged before leaving, and enter hospital or guardianship on the other side of the border under the admission procedures of that country, either compulsory or informal. On the other hand, if it is necessary to have powers of control over the patient while on the journey and immediately on arrival in the other country, the procedures described in sections 80 to 85 may be used. These sections define the categories of patients who may be moved without a break in the powers of detention or guardianship and

how they are to be treated as regards powers of detention, guardianship, and discharge after arriving in the receiving country.

Removal from England and Wales

262 The suggestion that a patient should be moved from a hospital in England and Wales may originate from the patient himself or his relatives or friends or from the hospital or other authority in whose care he is. Preliminary enquiries about arrangements for his care in the other country should be made before an approach is made to the Secretary of State whose authority for the removal is required under the relevant section of the Act. The views of the person exercising the functions of the nearest relative should if possible be ascertained and reported to the Secretary of State whenever it is desired to remove a patient under section 80 or 81.

Removal to England and Wales

263 When a patient who is detained under the equivalent of Part II of the Act is moved to England or Wales under section 82 or section 77 of the Mental Health (Scotland) Act 1984 or under a corresponding provision of the Channel Islands or Isle of Man legislation, he is to be treated on arrival as though admitted to hospital on an application made under sections 2 or 3 of the Act, or as though received into guardianship under sections 7 and 8. He will have a right of application to a Mental Health Review Tribunal under section 66(1) within 6 months of his transfer. The written authority for removal given by the appropriate authority at the patient's place of origin will be sent to the receiving hospital or guardian, and to the local social services authority if it is not the guardian and should be kept as the document authorising the patient's detention or guardianship in England and Wales. With it should be kept the record of the date of arrival at the hospital or other place where he is to reside, which is required by regulation 11. The managers of the hospital should, if reasonably practicable, inform the patient's nearest relative, if any, of the admission or guardianship.

264 The authority for detention or guardianship will expire if not renewed at the end of 6 months from that date under section 20 and all the other relevant provisions of Part II of the Act also apply. Section 92(3) and regulation 11 require the responsible medical officer (or nominated medical attendant) to record the form of mental disorder from which the

patient is suffering, in accordance with the classifications recognised under the Act in England and Wales, on form 32 as soon as possible after his arrival. In cases of reception into the guardianship of a person other than a local social services authority, the date of arrival is to be notified by the guardian to the responsible local social services authority, as well as the other notifications required under regulation 12. He must also inform the nearest relative, if any, as soon as reasonably practicable, of the patient's reception into guardianship.

265 When a patient who is moved to England and Wales under the provisions described in the previous paragraph was before removal treated as subject to a hospital order with or without a restriction order, he is to be treated on arrival as though admitted under the equivalent provision of Part III of the Act. Under section 69(2)(a) *such a patient has a right of application to the Mental Health Review Tribunal* within the first 6 months, unlike most other Part III patients. Regulation 11 requires the responsible medical officer to record the patient's mental classification on his arrival (if he is not subject to restriction on discharge) or (if he is so subject) when the restriction ceases to have effect.

266 When a restricted patient who has been conditionally discharged in Scotland under the equivalent of section 42 or 73 is moved to England and Wales under section 82A or 85A, or under section 77A of the Mental Health (Scotland) Act 1984, he is to be treated on arrival as if he were a restricted patient who had been conditionally discharged on the date of the transfer. He will have a right of application to a Mental Health Review Tribunal under section 75, 12 months after the date of transfer.

Removal of mentally ill aliens

267 Section 86 of the Mental Health Act empowers the Home Secretary to authorise the removal to any country abroad of a person who is neither a British citizen nor a Commonwealth citizen with the right of abode in the United Kingdom, who is receiving in-patient treatment for mental disorder in England and Wales or Northern Ireland and who is detained pursuant to an application for admission for treatment, a hospital order or an order or direction having the same effect as a hospital order. The Home Secretary must be satisfied that proper arrangements have been made for the patient's care or treatment in the country to which he is to

be moved, and *the proposal must have the approval of a Mental Health Review Tribunal.* In such cases the Home Secretary will exercise his discretionary power to refer the patient to a Tribunal. The Tribunal will be asked for advice whether removal would be in the best interests of the patient and whether proper arrangements have been made for his care or treatment.

268 Proposals for the removal of such a person from a hospital or mental nursing home should be made in the first place to the Home Office (Mental Health Unit, Queen Anne's Gate, London SW1H 9AT). Details should be given of any arrangements which have been or could be made for the patient's care and treatment in the receiving country. The Home Office will, in consultation with the Department of Health, decide whether authority under section 86 should be issued or whether the patient should be repatriated under other powers. Application to the Home Office will not be necessary if the patient, whether or not accompanied by an escort, is able and willing to travel without powers of detention, and suitable arrangements have been made.

269 The types of cases in which it might be appropriate to propose repatriation include:

a.   those where repatriation would be in the person's interest;

b.   those where the person has been in hospital in this country for a considerable period (6 months or more), where there is little prospect of a substantial improvement in his condition and where repatriation would not be detrimental to him.

270 Normally when a patient is removed from England and Wales under section 86 the authority for his detention ceases to have effect forthwith. But where the patient is subject to a hospital order together with a restriction order, they will remain in force so that they will apply to the patient if he should return before they would otherwise have expired.

Retaking of patients

271 Sections 87 and 89 permit patients who are absent without leave from mental hospitals or institutions in Northern Ireland, the Channel Islands or the Isle of Man to be retaken if found in England and Wales.

Equivalent provision in respect of patients from Scotland is made by section 84 of the Mental Health (Scotland) Act 1984. The persons authorised to retake such patients are approved social workers or constables in England and Wales, who may be asked to co-operate with the Scottish, Northern Ireland, or Island authorities in such cases. Section 88 permits patients from England and Wales to be retaken in Scotland, Northern Ireland, the Channel Islands or the Isle of Man as mentioned in para 75 of this memorandum. All these provisions are subject to any time limits which apply to the retaking of patients in the country from which the patient is absent.

272 Sections 87, 88 and 89 do not apply to patients under guardianship. The powers of guardians are in abeyance while a patient is not in the part of the United Kingdom in which the guardianship is in force. They revive if the patient returns while the authority for guardianship is still in force, ie if it has not lapsed under sections 18, 20 to 21B, or 22, or been discharged under section 23.

Miscellaneous functions of local authorities and the Secretary of State

Approved social workers

273 Section 114(1) requires a local social services authority to appoint a sufficient number of approved social workers to carry out the functions given to them by the Act. Section 114(2) provides that nobody can be appointed as an approved social worker unless the local social services authority has approved him as having appropriate competence in dealing with people who are suffering from mental disorder. In appointing people as approved social workers, the local social services authority must have regard to the directions issued by the Secretary of State in circular LAC (86) 15 (Welsh Office Circular 51/86) (section 114(3)).

Visiting patients

274 Local authorities have a duty to arrange visits to certain patients in hospital or nursing homes whether or not the patients concerned are being treated for mental disorder (section 116). Local authorities must also take such other steps in relation to these patients while they are in a hospital or nursing home as would be expected to be taken by the patient's parents. This section applies to:

a.   a child or young person who is in the care of a local authority by virtue of a care order within the meaning of the Children Act 1989, or in respect of whom the rights and powers of a parent are vested in a local authority by virtue of section 16 of the Social Work (Scotland) Act 1968.

b.   a person who is subject to the guardianship of a local social services authority under the 1983 Act (see paras 38-43) or the Mental Health (Scotland) Act 1984.

c.   a person the functions of whose nearest relative under the 1983 Act or the Mental Health (Scotland) Act 1984 are for the time being transferred to a local social services authority (see para 107-112).

After-care

275 Section 117 reinforces the duty which already exists under other legislation for health and social services authorities (in co-operation with relevant voluntary agencies) to provide after-care. It pinpoints three specific groups of detained patients whose discharge from hospital is to be followed by the provision of after-care services for as long as they are needed:

a.   persons who have been detained under section 3;

b.   persons who have been admitted to hospital in pursuance of a hospital order under section 37;

c.   persons who have been admitted to hospital in pursuance of a hospital direction under section 45A or a transfer direction under section 47 or 48.

276 Guidance on the discharge of mentally disordered people and their continuing care in the community is contained in Health Service Guideline (94)27 (Local Authority Social Services Letter (94)4).

277 An after-care form which is designed to be used for all patients discharged from psychiatric in-patient treatment, including those subject to section 117, was sent to relevant agencies by the Department of Health in February 1995.

Code of Practice

278 Section 118 requires the Secretary of State to prepare, publish and from time to time revise, a Code of Practice. The Code must include:

a.   guidance in relation to compulsory admissions to hospitals and mental nursing homes under the Act;

b.   guidance in relation to guardianship and after-care under supervision under the Act;

c.   guidance in relation to the medical treatment of patients suffering from mental disorder.

279 The Mental Health Act Commission is responsible for submitting proposals for revisions to the Code. In particular they may want to propose revisions to it when developments in professional practice, or particular issues where guidance is needed, have come to their attention. It will be noted that (c) is not confined to the treatment of detained patients. The Code does not have the force of law, but everyone involved in the care of mentally disordered patients, including treatment in the community, should have regard to it whenever it is relevant. Failure to do so could be evidence of bad practice.

280 Section 118(2) provides that the Code of Practice shall specify forms of medical treatment which give rise to special concern and should therefore only be given with consent and a second opinion (see para 216-219). Any forms of treatment specified in the Code would be in addition to those specified in the regulations made under section 57(1) (regulation 16), and the forms of treatment so specified should be treated as section 57 treatments. To date no such treatments have been specified in the Code.

281 The Secretary of State must consult bodies which appear to him to be concerned before he revises the Code of Practice. Any revision of the Code is subject to the approval of Parliament (section 118(3) and (4)).

The Mental Health Act Commission

282 The Mental Health Act Commission has been set up as a Special Health Authority by the Secretary of State, and like other health authorities it has to comply with directions from him, but otherwise it is independent in the performance of its functions, and in the advice it offers. Section 121(2) requires that the Secretary of State must direct the Commission to carry out certain functions listed there (see below). The Commission has been designated by an Order in Council under section 109(d) of the NHS Act 1977 as an authority subject to the Health Service Commissioner's jurisdiction.

283 The Secretary of State for Health and the Secretary of State for Wales are responsible for making appointments to the Commission. The membership of the Commission includes lawyers, nurses, psychologists, social workers, lay people and doctors. The members of the Commission together have a wide range of experience and knowledge of the issues involved in the compulsory admission and medical treatment of mental patients.

284 The functions which the Secretary of State has directed the Commission to perform on his behalf are:

a.   appointing medical practitioners and others for the purposes of the Consent to Treatment provisions (see paras 217-218 and 221). These appointed people may include Commissioners but there may be some who are not members of the Commission;

b.   carrying out the function described in section 61 (the review of treatment given only after a second opinion has been obtained) (see para 224);

c.   carrying out the functions described in section 120 (the visiting of patients and investigation of complaints) (see paras 290-293).

285 The Commission is also required by the Act to:

a.   produce a report every two years;

b.   review the decision to withhold a postal packet if an application is made to it to do so (section 121(7) and see para 313).

286 The Commission, under the guidance of its Management Board, also produces written guidance on issues relating to the administration of the Act and, in accordance with its Establishment Order in 1983, prepares proposals for the Code of Practice.

287 The Commission can also be directed by the Secretary of State, after consultation, to look at any matter relating to the care and treatment of patients not detained under the Act (section 121(4)). The Code of Practice (see above) does in any case cover treatment for mental disorder in general.

288 The Commission's functions are quite separate from those of Mental Health Review Tribunals (see Part V) which determine whether a patient should continue to be detained. The Commission has no power to discharge a patient.

289 The Orders and regulations concerning the functions, establishment, and constitution of the Commission are the Mental Health Act Commission regulations 1983 (Statutory Instrument 1983 No 894 (as amended by SI 1990 No 1331 and SI 1995 No 2630)), the Mental Health Act Commission (Establishment and Constitution) Order 1983 (Statutory Instrument 1983 No 892), The Health Service Commissioner for England (Mental Health Act Commission) Order 1983 (Statutory Instrument 1983 No 1114) and The Mental Health (Amendment) Act 1982 (Commencement No 1) Order 1983 (Statutory Instrument 1983 No 890 (c 24)).

The general protection of detained patients

290 Section 120 confers certain duties on the Secretary of State in connection with the general protection of detained patients. Section 121 provides that those duties are to be carried out by the Mental Health Act Commission. Accordingly section 120(1) requires the Commission to keep under review the exercise of the powers conferred by the Act in relation to the detention of patients. The Commission is also required to make arrangements for persons authorised by it to visit and interview in private patients detained in hospitals and mental nursing homes. The authorised persons may also investigate any complaint which a detained patient thinks has not been dealt with satisfactorily by the hospital managers or any other complaint concerning the use of powers given by the Act. The Commission can investigate a complaint made by an ex-patient which he does not feel has been satisfactorily dealt with by the managers as long as it relates to a period of detention under the Act or any complaint made by a relative or friend of a patient, or by another person, in relation to that patient or ex-patient. Where such a complaint is made by a Member of Parliament the Commission are required to inform him of the results of any investigation carried out.

291 The Commission will direct any problems the detained patients have to the hospital managers or to other appropriate channels, but is also

able to take up any matters where patients feel their grievance has not been resolved satisfactorily. The Commission does not replace or duplicate the work of other individuals and bodies who are able to help patients with their problems, for example hospital managers, Community Health Councils, voluntary organisations, Members of Parliament and the Health Service Commissioner. Persons carrying out an investigation on behalf of the Commission can discontinue it if they consider it right to do so (for example because it would be more suitably investigated by the Health Service Commissioner), but will try to ensure that detained patients are helped with particular problems by the most appropriate person or body (section 120(2)).

292 Any person authorised by the Commission has the right of access to detained patients and their records at any reasonable time. In the case of mental nursing homes this is achieved by virtue of section 120(4). In the case of NHS hospitals this is achieved by the direction issued by the Secretary of State, notified in circular HC(83)19, which also ensures that this happens in Special Hospitals. Authorised persons may visit, interview, and in the case of medical practitioners examine, in private, any detained patient. They may also require the production of and inspect any records relating to the detention or treatment of a detained patient (including admission documents, medical notes, records of seclusion etc).

293 As well as looking at individual patients' complaints, the Commission also reviews the way in which the powers of detention are being exercised and monitors the working of the consent to treatment provisions. Members of the Commission will regularly visit every hospital or mental nursing home where a patient is detained, with more frequent visits to Special Hospitals. Commissioners will usually be able and willing to give notice of their intention to visit a hospital or mental nursing home, but they do not have to, and on occasions may prefer to visit unannounced. It is an offence under section 129 to refuse an authorised person access to a patient or to records, or in any way obstruct him in carrying out his functions.

High Security Hospitals

294 High security, or "special hospitals", are required to be provided by the Secretary of State for Health under section 4 of the National Health

Service Act 1977. There are three such hospitals: Broadmoor, Rampton and Ashworth. Three special health authorities have been established to manage these hospitals; see the Ashworth, Broadmoor and Rampton Hospitals (Establishment and Constitution) Order 1996 (SI 1996 No 488). By virtue of regulation 2 of the Ashworth, Broadmoor and Rampton (Functions and Membership) regulations 1996 (SI 1996 No 489) each of these authorities is directed to exercise on behalf of the Secretary of State his functions under the 1983 Act as "the managers" of the relevant hospital. The high security hospitals provide the same range of therapeutic services as general psychiatric hospitals but they are intended by virtue of the National Health Service Act 1977 for the treatment of patients who are detained under the Mental Health Act and who, in the opinion of the Secretary of State, require this treatment under special security because of their dangerous, violent or criminal propensities. The regimes of care and observation are such that they can only be justified when the highest level of security is required and no lesser degree of security would provide a reasonable safeguard to the public.

Miscellaneous and supplementary provisions

Informal and emergency admissions

295 Informal admission should be the normal mode of admission to hospital when patients consent to admission and treatment. Informal admission should also be used when patients lack the capacity to consent if they are not unwilling to be admitted and treated (see section 131 and *In Re L [1998]*).

296 The attention of Health Authorities is drawn to the fact that section 140 places a statutory duty on them to notify local social services authorities, wholly or partly in their area, of hospitals which have arrangements for admitting emergencies. This duty will be met if the Health Authority makes arrangements for social services authorities to be kept aware of psychiatric catchment areas for particular hospitals within the Region, with suitable notes explaining, for example, where the catchment area for elderly patients differs from that for younger patients. (Health Authorities must also provide the courts with information about hospital places if requested. See para 173.)

The duty of hospital managers to provide information

297 Sections 132 and 133 place a duty upon hospital managers to provide certain information to detained patients and their nearest relatives. Section 132(1) places a duty on hospital and mental nursing home managers to take such steps as are practicable to ensure that a detained patient understands:

a.   which section of the Act for the time being authorises his detention and the effects of that section;

b.   his right to apply to a Mental Health Review Tribunal (if applicable).

This information must be given as soon as practicable after the commencement of the patient's detention and as soon as practicable after a different section of the Act is used to authorise his detention. In practice this will mean that the patient will have to be told immediately if he is detained for 72 hours or less. When the responsible medical officer, nurse or other professional gives this information to the patient he should be as helpful as possible, and try to explain to the patient any points he does not appear to understand. He should also hand the patient the written statement required by section 132(1) and (3) (see para 300).

298 Section 132(2) places a further duty on hospital managers to take such steps as are practicable to ensure that a detained patient understands the effect, so far as it is relevant to him, of the following sections of the Act:

a.   sections 23, 25 and 66(1)(g) which deal with the power of the responsible medical officer, the hospital managers and the nearest relative to discharge him (see paras 102-105);

b.   Part IV of the Act which deals with consent to treatment (see paras 212-230);

c.   section 118 which deals with the Code of Practice (see paras 278-281);

d.   section 120 which deals with the general protection of patients (see para 290-293);

e.   section 134 which deals with patients' correspondence (see para 303-311);

299 In particular the intention is that the patient should understand the means by which his detention can be ended and the various safeguards from which he benefits including those concerning consent to treatment. The patient should also be told about any legal aid schemes which could help him obtain representation for a Mental Health Review Tribunal. Transferred patients should be told about any special Mental Health Review Tribunal rights.

300 The information required under sections 132(1) and 132(2) must be given both orally and in writing, and the information given in writing must, except where the patient otherwise requests, be given to the nearest relative within a reasonable time. Leaflets, containing the minimum information to be given to the patient, are produced by the Department of Health and in Wales by the Welsh Office in order to assist the hospital managers fulfil their responsibilities under the Act (see Appendix 4).

301 When a patient is discharged from detention, or the authority for his detention expires, this fact should be made clear to him, whether he wishes to leave hospital or to stay on as an informal patient.

Duty of managers to inform nearest relative of discharge

302 Section 133 requires that where a patient is to be discharged from detention other than by an order of the nearest relative, the person (if any) appearing to be the nearest relative should be informed, within 7 days if practicable, of the patient's discharge, unless the patient or the relative has asked that such information should not be given.

Patients' correspondence

303 Section 134 provides power for detained patients' incoming or out-going mail to be inspected and withheld. There are no restrictions on informal patients' correspondence. A 'postal packet' has the same meaning in section 134 as it does in the Post Office Act 1953 which is: 'a letter, postcard, reply postcard, newspaper, printed packet or parcel and every packet or article transmissible by post (which includes a telegram).'

304 A postal packet addressed by any detained patient may be withheld from the Post Office if the person to whom it is addressed has asked that he should receive no correspondence from that patient (section 134(1)(a)). A request from a person that correspondence addressed to him by the patient should be withheld must be in writing, and must be given to the hospital managers, the responsible medical officer or the Secretary of State. Any power to withhold a postal packet in that section applies also to any item contained in a postal packet. If appropriate, an item from a packet can be withheld and the rest of the packet forwarded to the addressee (see section 134(4)).

305 Section 134(1)(b) applies only to Broadmoor, Ashworth and Rampton Hospitals and provides that a postal packet can be withheld from the Post Office if it is likely to cause distress to the person to whom it is addressed or to any other person who is not on the staff of the hospital or to cause danger to any person. It is intended that this power should be used to withhold for example, threatening letters, letters to victims of crime, or dangerous objects. Section 132(2) also applies only to Broadmoor, Ashworth and Rampton Hospitals. It allows the managers of these hospitals (or a member of staff appointed by them) to withhold a postal packet from a patient if they believe it is necessary to do so in the interests of the safety of the patient or for the protection of other persons.

306 Section 134(3) modifies the powers mentioned in paragraph 305 above so that postal packets cannot be withheld if they are addressed to a patient by or on behalf of certain people or bodies, or if sent by the patient to those people or bodies.

The people or bodies concerned are:

a.   any Government Minister or Member of Parliament;

b.   the Master or any other officer of the Court of Protection or any of the Lord Chancellor's Visitors;

c.   the Parliamentary Commissioner, the Health Service Commissioner for England or for Wales or a Local Commissioner;

d.   a Mental Health Review Tribunal;

e.   a Health Authority, Special Health Authority, local social services authority, Community Health Council or probation committee;

f.   the managers of the hospital where the patient is detained;

g.   the patient's legal adviser (if legally qualified and instructed by the patient to act for him);

h.   the European Commission of Human Rights or the European Court of Human Rights.

307 The managers of a hospital, or a person appointed by them, may inspect or open any postal packet to see whether it is one to which sections 134(1) and (2) apply and if so, whether it or anything contained in

it, should be withheld. In hospitals other than special hospitals it will not be necessary to open correspondence, only to look at the address. In special hospitals it may be necessary to open both outgoing and incoming letters to determine whether section 134(1) or (2) apply. (Postal packets should only be opened when there is a suspicion that these sections do apply.)

Procedure for inspecting correspondence

308 Regulation 17 describes the procedure which should be followed if a postal packet is inspected and opened. Inspection alone does not have to be recorded: this includes cases where the contents can be read without opening (ie in the case of a postcard). If a packet is opened but nothing is withheld, the person who opened the packet must place a notice in the packet stating:

a.   that the packet has been opened and inspected;

b.   that nothing has been withheld;

c.   his name and the name of the hospital.

309 Where a postal packet or item contained in it is withheld, a record must be made in a register kept for the purpose by the person who withheld it of:

a.   the fact that the package or item in it has been withheld;

b.   the date and the grounds on which it was withheld;

c.   the name of the appointed person who withheld it;

d.   a description of the item withheld.

If anything in a packet is withheld, but the package is allowed to go on to the addressee, a notice should be placed in the packet stating:

a.   that the packet has been opened and inspected and an item withheld;

b.   the grounds on which the item has been withheld;

c.   the name of the appointed person who withheld it;

d.   a description of the item withheld;

e.   the effect of sub-sections 7 and 8 of section 121.

((b) and (e) do not apply in section 134(i)(a) cases)

310 Where a whole postal packet is withheld, in a special hospital the addressee must be sent a notice stating (b), (c), (d) and (e) above and the fact that the packet has been withheld (see section 134(b) and regulation 17). Any item withheld must be kept safe for a period of six months after which it should, if practicable, be returned to the sender. The police should be informed if a dangerous item is withheld.

Mental Health Act Commission's power to review a decision to withhold post

311 Section 121(7) gives the Mental Health Act Commission power to review any decision to withhold a postal packet under sections 134(1)(b) or (2) provided an application to review such a decision is made within six months of the receipt of the written notice. The applicant should provide the Commission with a copy of the written notice. In the case of outgoing mail it is only the special hospital patient who may apply, but in the case of incoming mail, the special hospital patient or the sender may apply. When reviewing a decision to withhold a postal packet the Commission may inspect documents and evidence (including the withheld item) which it reasonably requires. The Commission has the power to release the withheld item to the addressee (section 121(8)).

Managers' power to appoint staff to inspect post

312 The managers of a hospital can appoint such staff or categories of staff as they think fit to inspect and withhold post. It is expected that the decision to withhold post would be made in consultation with the responsible medical officer.

Assistance from the police to retake patients or to remove them to a place of safety

313 The police are included among the people authorised to retake patients who are absent without leave from the hospital where they are liable to be detained or from the place where they are required by their guardian to live (section 18). They are also included among the people authorised by sections 137 and 138 to retake patients who escape while being conveyed from one place to another, or who escape from a place of safety or custody under the Act.

314 Section 135 provides powers of entry to premises on a magistrate's warrant, based on information supplied, by an approved social worker to obtain access to a patient in the circumstances described in section 135(1)(a) and (b). Section 135(4) requires that when a constable executes a warrant under subsection (1) he must be accompanied by a doctor and an approved social worker. The doctor will be able to advise whether the patient should be removed to a place of safety pending an application under Part II of the Act. A place of safety is defined as residential accommodation provided by a local social services authority (under Part III of the National Assistance Act 1948) a hospital, police station, mental nursing home, residential home for mentally disordered people or any other suitable place where the occupier is willing temporarily to receive the patient.

315 If the patient is removed to a place of safety he may be kept there for not more than 72 hours while other arrangements are made. Only in exceptional circumstances should a police station be used as a place of safety. If a police station is used, the patient should remain there for no longer than a few hours while an approved social worker makes the necessary arrangements for his removal elsewhere, either informally or under Part II of the Act.

316 Section 135(2) provides for the issue of a warrant to enter premises and take or retake a patient who has escaped or who is absent without leave. When a constable executes the warrant he may be accompanied by a doctor or any other person who is already authorised to retake the patient. The person who is authorised to retake the patient should normally accompany the constable and then take the patient direct to the hospital or place where he is required to live.

317 The police also have the power under section 136 to remove to a place of safety a person whom they find in a place to which the public have access who appears to be suffering from mental disorder and to be in immediate need of care or control in his own interests or for the protection of others. The person can be detained in the place of safety (as defined in section 135(6)) (see para 314) for up to 72 hours so that he can be examined by a doctor and interviewed by an approved social worker in order that any necessary arrangements can be made for his treatment or care.

Detention of MPs and Members of the House of Lords

318 Section 141(1) provides that when a member of the House of Commons is detained under the Act on the ground that he is suffering from mental illness the following bodies or persons all have a duty to inform the Speaker of the House of Commons at the Palace of Westminster, London SW1 that the detention of that MP has been authorised:

a. the court, authority or person who made the order or application for detention;

b. the registered medical practitioners making the medical recommendations;

c. the managers of the hospital or mental nursing home or other place where the MP is detained.

319 There is no similar provision in the Act for members of the House of Lords but House of Lords Standing Order 77 requires a court or authority ordering the imprisonment or restraint of a member of the House of Lords to give written notice to the Clerk of the Parliaments. Where a member of the House of Lords is detained under the Act, the managers of the hospital or mental nursing home where that member is detained should inform the Clerk of the Parliaments, House of Lords, SW1 in writing of the section of the Act under which that member is detained and the date of his detention. The Clerk should also be informed when the member of the House of Lords is discharged or given leave of absence, or if he absents himself without leave. Where the member of the House of Lords is sent from a court or transferred from prison, the court or prison will have informed the Clerk of the Parliaments but when that member is discharged or given leave of absence, or if he absents himself from the hospital or nursing home without leave, it will be for the managers to inform the Clerk.

Protection for acts done in pursuance of the Act

320 Section 139 gives protection against litigation to persons acting in pursuance of the Act or any regulations or rules made under the Act so long as the act in question was not done in bad faith or without reasonable care. The section also covers acts purporting to be done in pursu-

ance of the Act, and acts done under other legislation relating to the Court of Protection. Criminal proceedings against staff require the consent of the Director of Public Prosecutions and civil proceedings require the consent of the High Court. Section 139 does not apply to proceedings against the Secretary of State or against a Health Authority, a Special Health Authority or a NHS trust.

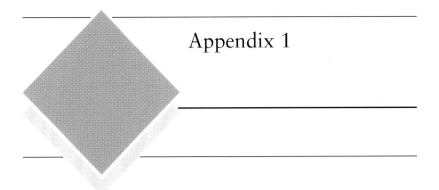

Appendix 1

Address of Mental Health Act Commission Office

Mental Health Act Commission
Maid Marian House
56 Hounds Gate
Nottingham NG1 6BG

Tel: 0115 943 7100
Fax: 0115 943 7101

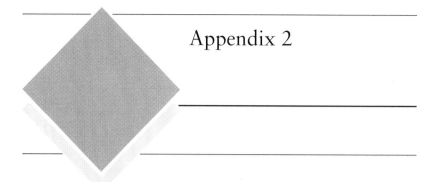

Appendix 2

Addresses of the Mental Health Review Tribunals and the areas they will cover with effect from 1 August 1998 when the Mental Health Review Tribunals (Regions) Order comes into force

Nottingham Mental Health Review
Tribunal Secretariat
Spur A Block 5
Government Buildings
Chalfont Drive
Western Boulevard
Nottingham NG8 3RZ

This office covers:
East Midlands and Northern
Region
Rampton Hospital

Tel: 0115 929 4222
Fax: 0115 942 8303

Liverpool Mental Health Review
Tribunal Secretariat
Cressington House
249 St Mary's Road
Garston
Liverpool L19 ONF

This office covers:
West Midlands and the North
West Region
Ashworth Hospital

Tel: 0151 494 0095
Fax: 0151 427 0133

London South Mental Health
Review Tribunal
Secretariat
Hinchley Wood
Block 3, Crown Offices
Kingston-By-Pass Road
Surbiton
Surrey KT6 5QN

Tel: 0181 268 4520
Fax: 0181 268 4532

This office covers:
South and West Region
Broadmoor Hospital

London North Mental Health
Review Tribunal Secretariat
Canons Park
Government Buildings
Honeypot Lane
Stanmore
Middlesex HA7 1AY

Tel: 0171 972 3734
Fax: 0171 972 3731

This office covers:
Central and Anglia Region

Welsh Mental Health Review
Tribunal Secretariat
4th Floor
Crown Building
Cathays Park
Cardiff CF1 3NQ

Tel: 01222 825328
Fax: 01222 825671

This office covers:
Wales

Appendix 3

Legal aid areas and offices

London (Areas: No.1,13 &14)
29-37 Red Lion Street
London WC1R 4PP
Tel: 0171 813 5300

**South Eastern, Brighton
(Area No.2)**
3rd and 4th Floors
Invicta House
Trafalgar Place
Cheapside
Brighton BB1 4FR
Tel: 01273 699622

Southern, Reading (Area No.3)
80 Kings Road
Reading RG1 4LT
Tel: 0118-9589696

**North Western, Manchester
(Area No.7)**
2nd Floor
Elizabeth House
16, St. Peter's Square
Manchester M2 3DA
Tel: 0161-228 1200

South Western, Bristol (Area No.4)
33-35 Queen Square
Bristol BS1 4LU
Tel: 0117 921-480

South Wales, Cardiff (Area No.5)
Marland House
Central Square
Cardiff CF1 1PE
Tel: 01222-388971

**West Midlands, Birmingham
(Area No.6)**
Centre-City Podium
5 Hill Street
Birmingham B5 4UD
Tel: 0121-632 6541

Eastern, Cambridge (Area No.11)
Kett House
Station Road
Cambridge CB1 2JT
Tel: 01223-366511

Northern, Newcastle (Area No.8)
Eagle Star House
Fenkle Street
Newcastle upon Tyne
NE1 5RU
Tel: 0191-232 3461

North Eastern, Leeds (Area No.9)
City House
New Station Street
Leeds LS1 4JS
Tel: 0113-244 2851

Chester & North Wales, Chester (Area No.12)
Pepper House, 2nd Floor
Pepper Row
Chester CG1 1DW
Tel: 01244-315455

Merseyside, Liverpool (Area No.15)
Cavern Walks
8 Mathew Street
Liverpool L26 RE
Tel: 0151-236 8371

East Midlands, Nottingham (Area No.10)
1st Floor
Fothergill House
16 King Street
Nottingham NG1 2AS
Tel: 0115-955 9600

Area	Legal Aid Area & Office	Area	Legal Aid Area &Office
Allerdale	8a, Newcastle-Upon-Tyne	Devon	4a, Bristol
		Dorset	3b, Reading
Barnet	14, London	Dudley	6b, Birmingham
Barrow-in-Furness	7b, Manchester	Durham	8b, Newcastle-Upon-Tyne
Bath & North East Somerset	4b, Bristol	Dyfed	5, Cardiff
Bedfordshire	11a, Cambridge	Ealing	1, London
Berkshire	3a, Reading	East Riding of Yorkshire	9b, Leeds
Bexley	1, London		
Birmingham	6b, Birmingham	East Staffordshire	12b, Chester
Blackburn	7b, Manchester	East Sussex	2, Brighton
Blackpool	15, Liverpool	Eden	8a, Newcastle-Upon-Tyne
Bournmouth	3b, Reading		
Brecknock	5, Cardiff	Enfield	14, London
Brent	14, London	Essex	11b, Cambridge
Brighton & Hove	2, Brighton	Frome	4b, Bristol
Bristol	4b, Bristol	Fylde	15, Liverpool
Bromley	1, London	Glastonbury	4b, Bristol
Buckinghamshire	3a, Reading	Gloustershire	4b, Bristol
Burnley	7b, Manchester	Greenwich	1, London
Cambridgeshire	11a, Cambridge	Gwent	5, Gwent
Camden	13, London	Gwynedd	12a, Chester
Cannock Chase	6b, Birmingham	Hackney	13, London
Carlisle	8a, Newcastle-Upon-Tyne	Hambleton	8b, Newcastle
		Hammersmith	14, London
Cheshire	12b, Chester	Hampshire	3b, Reading
Chorley	7b, Manchester	Haringey	14, London
Clywde	12a, Chester	Harrogate	9a, Leeds
Copeland	8a, Newcastle-Upon-Tyne	Harrow	14, London
		Hartlepool	8b, Newcastle-Upon-Tyne
Cornwall	4a, Bristol		
Coventry	6a, Birmingham	Havering	13, London
Craven	9a, Leeds	Hereford & Worcester	6a, Birmingham
Croydon	1, London		
Darlington	8b, Newcastle-Upon-Tyne	Hertfordshire	11b, Cambridge
		Hillingdon	14, London
Deane	4a, Bristol	Hounslow	1, London
Derby	10a, Nottingham	Hull	9b, Leeds
Derbyshire	10a, Nottingham	Hynburn	7b, Manchester

Area	Legal Aid Area & Office	Area	Legal Aid Area & Office
Isle of Wight	3b, Reading	Portsmouth	3b, Reading
Islington	13, London	Preston	15, Liverpool
Kensington & Chelsea	14, London	Radnor	5, Cardiff
		Redbridge	13, London
Kent	2, Brighton	Redcar & Cleveland	8b, Newcastle-Upon-Tyne
Kingston	1, London		
Lambeth	1, London	Ribble Valley	7b, Manchester
Lancaster	7b, Manchester	Richmond	1, London
Leicester	10, Cambridge	Richmondshire	8b, Newcastle-Upon-Tyne
Leicestershire	10b, Cambridge		
Lewisham	1, London	Rossendale	7b, Manchester
Lichfield	6b, Birmingham	Rutland	10b, Cambridge
Lincolnshire	10a, Nottingham	Rydale	8b, Newcastle-Upon-Tyne
Luton	11a, Cambridge		
Manchester (Greater)	7a, Manchester	Sandwell	6b, Birmingham
		Scarborough	8b, Newcastle-Upon-Tyne
Merseyside	15, Liverpool		
Merton	1, London	Sedgemoor	4a, Bristol
Middlesbrough	8b, Newcastle-Upon-Tyne	Selby	9a, Leeds
		Shepton Mallet	4b, Bristol
Mid Glamorgan	5, Cardiff	Shropshire	12b, Chester
Milton Keynes	3a, Reading	Solihull	6a, Birmingham
Montgomery	12a, Chester	South Glamorgan	5, Cardiff
Newcastle-under-Lyme	12b, Chester	South Gloustershire	4b, Bristol
		Southampton	3b, Reading
Newham	13, London	South Lakeland	7b, Manchester
Norfolk	11a, Cambridge	South Ribble	15, Liverpool
Northamptonshire	10b, Cambridge	South Stafford-shire	6, Birmingham
North East Lincolnshire	10a, Nottingham		
		South Yorkshire	9, Leeds
North Lincolnshire	10a, Nottingham	Southwark	1, London
Northumberland	8a, Newcastle-Upon-Tyne	Stafford	12b, Chester
		Staffordshire Moors	12b, Chester
North West Somerset	4b, Bristol		
		Stock-on-Trent	8b, Newcastle-Upon-Tyne
Nottinghamshire	10a, Nottingham		
Oxfordshire	3a, Reading	Suffolk	12b, Chester
Pendle	7b, Manchester	Surrey	11a, Cambridge
Poole	3b, Reading		

Area	Legal Aid Area & Office	Area	Legal Aid Area & Office
Sutton	2, Brighton	Warwickshire	4b, Bristol
Tamworth	6b, Birmingham	Wells	5, Cardiff
Taunton	4a, Bristol	West Glamorgan	15, Liverpool
Thamesdown	4b, Bristol	West Lancashire	14, London
The City of London	13, London	Westminster	2, Brighton
		West Sussex	9a, Leeds
Tower Hamlets	13, London	West Yorkshire	4b, Bristol
Tyne & Wear	8a, Newcastle-Upon-Tyne	Wiltshire	6b, Birmingham
		Wolverhampton	15, Liverpool
Walsall	6b, Birmingham	Wyre	4a, Bristol
Waltham Forest	1, London	Yeovil	4a, Bristol
Wandsworth	6a, Birmingham	York	9a Leeds

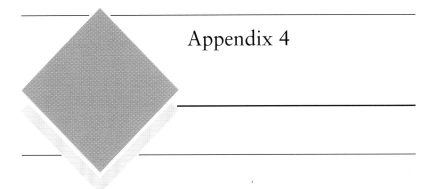

Appendix 4

Mental Health Act 1983 Patients' leaflets and statutory forms

The relevant section of the Mental Health Act 1983 appears in bold type after each entry

The Mental Health Act 1983 leaflets are non-statutory and are produced by the Department of Health and published by the Stationery
Office. Most leaflets have been translated into Bengali, Chinese,
Gujarati, Hindi, Urdu, Punjabi, Polish and Vietnamese. In Wales
leaflets are available in Welsh. Copies can be purchased from:

The Stationery Office
Broadway
Chadderton
Oldham
OL9 9QH

Mental Health Act 1983 Statutory Forms

The Mental Health Act 1983 section number appears in bold type after each entry

	Form Number
APPLICATIONS BY APPROVED SOCIAL WORKERS	
For admission for assessment S2	2
For emergency admission for assessment S4	6
For admission for treatment S3	9
For guardianship S7	18
APPLICATIONS BY NEAREST RELATIVE	
For admission for assessment S2	1
For emergency admission for assessment S4	5
For admission for treatment S3	8
For guardianship S7	17
MEDICAL RECOMMENDATIONS	
For admission for assessment S2	4
For emergency admission for assessment S4	7
For admission for treatment S3	11
For reception into guardianship S7	20
For transfer from guardianship to hospital S19	29
JOINT MEDICAL RECOMMENDATIONS	
For admission for assessment S2	3
For admission for treatment S3	10
For reception into guardianship S7	19
For transfer from guardianship to hospital S19	28
HOSPITAL REPORTS	
On a hospital in-patient S5(2)	12
Barring discharge by nearest relative S25	36
(see also Discharge)	(see also Form 34)

HOSPITAL RECORDS

CLASSIFICATION OF PATIENT

RECLASSIFICATION OF PATIENT

DISCHARGE BY NEAREST RELATIVE

RENEWAL OF AUTHORITY

CONSENT TO TREATMENT

AUTHORITY FOR TRANSFER OF A PATIENT

AFTER-CARE UNDER SUPERVISION

Application **S25B** or **S25J**	1S
Medical Recommendation **S25B**	2S
Approved Social Worker's Recommendation **S25B**	3S
Reclassification of a Patient **S25F**	4S
Renewal **S25G**	5S
Directing Termination **S25H**	6S

Copies of the forms can also be purchased from the Stationery Office at the above address.

The leaflets and forms can be re-produced locally.

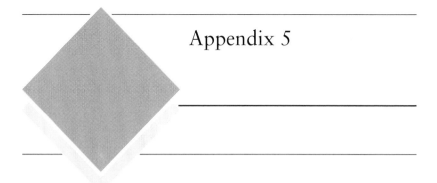

Appendix 5

Mental Health Act 1983: Part VI

Procedural guide on the removal of detained patients to and from Scotland and Northern Ireland (Paragraphs 236-247)

This is a brief summary only, acting as an aide-memoire; the advice cannot be authoritative in matters of law. Where doubt exists regarding correct procedure, legal advice should be obtained.

1   **Informal Patients** There are no formal requirements where an informal patient transfers to or from Scotland or Northern Ireland, but confirmation should be obtained that a receiving hospital is content with the arrangements and that the patient is willing to go.

2   **Conditionally Discharged Patients** Restricted patients living in the community subject to conditional discharge may be transferred between jurisdictions in the UK under the provisions of schedule 3 to the Crime (Sentences) Act 1997 and under sections 80A, 81A, and 82A of the Mental Health Act 1983 and from Scotland under section 77A and 80A of the Mental Health (Scotland) Act 1984.

This can be done where the patient wishes it, and where the relevant Secretary of State (the Home Secretary in England) or Minister responsible for the patient's supervision agrees that it is in (his or her) interests. Where a conditionally discharged person is transferred to England his conditional discharge will be treated as if it had taken place on the date of transfer; but any restriction order in force before transfer will expire on the date it would have expired if the person had not been transferred.

Supervisors should initially approach the caseworker dealing with the patient in the Home Office Mental Health Unit.

3   **Transfer of a Detained Patient from England to Scotland or Northern Ireland.** The Act provides that such a transfer can take place only where:

a.   a transfer is in the interests of the patient;

b.   arrangements have been made for admission and

c.   the Secretary of State has so authorised the transfer; and

d.   the patient is not subject to outstanding proceedings and is not being held under section 35, 36, or 38 of the Mental Health Act 1983.

4   **Transfer to Scotland or Northern Ireland of patients other than restricted patients** (Mental Health Act 1983, sections 2, 3 and 37 or 47 without an order or direction restricting discharge)

Once transfer has been agreed in principle between the sending and receiving hospitals, the sending hospital should write or fax to:

Health Services Directorate
Area 328
Department of Health
Wellington House
133-155 Waterloo Road
London SE1 8UG
Tel: (0171) 972 4515
Fax: (0171) 972 4147/4495

The sending hospital should include the following details:

a.   patient's full name and date of birth

b.   section of the Act under which he is detained

c.   the name of the doctor presently responsible for the patient

d.   name of the receiving hospital

e.   name of doctor agreeing to receive the patient

f.   reasons why transfer is considered to be in the patient's best interests.

Sufficient time should be allowed for arrangements to be checked with the receiving Government Department and for the written authority of the Secretary of State (for Health) to be issued. It will speed up matters if a copy of a letter from the proposed receiving hospital confirming willingness to accept the patient can be supplied.

5   **Transfer to Scotland or Northern Ireland of a restricted patient** Mental Health Act 1983, sections 37 and 41 and 45A and 47 and 48 with 49; also, patients detained under the Criminal Procedure (Insanity) Act 1964 as amended by the Criminal Procedure (Insanity and Unfitness to Plead) Act 1991.

Full details of the proposed transfer should be sent to:

Mental Health Unit
Home Office
Queen Anne's Gate
London
SW1H 9AT

6   **General Matters**

The escort accompanying the patient must take with the patient the documents authorising detention of the patient under the Mental Health Act 1983 and the formal authority for transfer.

7   **Transfer from Scotland or Northern Ireland of a Detained Patient**

Before finalising arrangements for reception, confirm that the sending hospital has sought formal authority for the transfer from the Scottish Office Department of Health or the Department of Health and Social Services, Northern Ireland, as appropriate. The authority of the appropriate Minister should accompany the other detention documents to be delivered to the hospital managers on the patient's arrival. The Home Office will wish to be involved at an early stage in the case of any restricted patient who will be subject to restrictions on discharge after transfer.

When the patient is admitted, Mental Health Form 33 must be completed on behalf of the managers. The responsible medical officer must, following his assessment of the patient, record on Form 32 (Mental Health Act 1983) the nature of the mental disorder (mental illness, severe mental impairment, mental impairment, and/or psychopathic disorder) from which the patient is suffering. Practitioners should note that psychopathic disorder is excluded from the definition of mental disorder under the Mental Health (Northern Ireland) Order 1986 (article 3(2)) and under the Mental Health (Scotland) Act 1984 (Section 17(1)(a)(i)).

The patient and nearest relative must be told of any rights of application, or to request a reference, to the Mental Health Review Tribunal, and the managers of the hospital must also give relevant information as indicated by Section 132 of the Mental Health Act 1983.

8 Transfers to and from Scotland or Northern Ireland - a brief guide to the corresponding provisions of the relevant legislation

i. **Patients transferred to England and Wales from Scotland or Northern Ireland**

When transferred into a hospital in England or Wales the patient is treated as having been admitted under an application, or order or direction made, on the date of admission to hospital in England or Wales (eg detention under section 3 lasts for six months from admission). Persons detained under respective sections of the Mental Health (Northern Ireland) Order or Mental Health (Scotland) Act 1984 appertaining to detention by virtue of a transfer direction while serving a sentence of imprisonment shall be treated as if the sentence had been imposed by a court in England or Wales. Where such a person prior to transfer to England and Wales was subject to an order or direction restricting his discharge, being an order or direction of limited duration, that direction shall expire on the date on which it would have expired if he had not been so transferred to England and Wales.

The patient will be liable to be detained under the provisions of the Mental Health Act 1983 corresponding to those under which he was detained under the Mental Health (Scotland) Act 1984 or Northern Ireland Order. (See Section 77 of the 1984 Act and Section 82 of the Mental Health Act 1983.) The commonest corresponding provisions are set out in paragraph 9.

ii. Patients transferred to Scotland or Northern Ireland from England and Wales

On arrival the patient will be liable to be detained under the provisions of the relevant Scottish or Northern Ireland legislation corresponding to the particular section of the Mental Health Act 1983 under which the patient was being detained in England or Wales. There is, however, an in-patient provision a provision in relation to section 80 (4) of the Mental Health Act 1983 which requires that a person detained by virtue of an application for admission for assessment under the 1983 Act (section 2) is, on admission to a hospital in Scotland, treated as if he had been admitted on that day to the hospital in Scotland on an emergency recommendation under the Mental Health (Scotland) Act 1984 (section 24).

9 Corresponding Provisions of the Relevant Legislation

The following information is given as guidance only. It should not be interpreted as authoritative. Legal advice must be sought in cases of doubt over correct procedure.

Mental Health (Scotland) Act 1984/ Criminal Procedure (Scotland) Act 1995	Mental Health (Northern Ireland) Order 1986	Mental Health Act 1983 (England and Wales)
Section 18*	Article 4	Section 2
Section 24†		Section 4
Section 18	Article 12	Section 3
Section 58 of the Criminal Procedure (Scotland) Act 1995, restrictions on discharge	Article 44 without restrictions on discharge	Section 37 without restrictions on discharge
Section 58 of the Criminal Procedure (Scotland) Act 1995 with a further order under Section 59 restricting discharge	Article 44 with restrictions under Article 47	Section 37 with restrictions on discharge under Section 41

Mental Health (Scotland) Act 1984/ Criminal Procedure (Scotland) Act 1995	Mental Health (Northern Ireland) Order 1986	Mental Health Act 1983 (England and Wales)
Section 57(2)(a) of the Criminal Procedure (Scotland) Act 1995 following a finding of insanity in bar of trial or aquitted on account of insanity **without** restrictions		(Home office advice will need to be sought an equivalent provisions)
Section 57(2)(b) of the Criminal Procedure (Scotland) Act 1995 following a finding of insanity in bar of trial or aquitted on account of insanity **with** restrictions		(Home Office advice will need to be sought on equivalent provisions)
Section 71 (transfer from prison) without restrictions on discharge	Article 53 (transfer of prisoners) without restrictions on discharge	Section 47
Section 71 transfer from prison with restrictions under Section 72	Article 53 with restrictions under Article 55	Section 47 with restrictions under Section 49

*   Section 18 of the Mental Health (Scotland) Act 1984 is not the exact equivalent of Section 2 of the Mental Health Act 1983 but will suffice for the purposes of transfer.

† Section 24 of the Mental Health (Scotland) Act 1984 is only a recommendation and not an application for admission and is therefore not the exact equivalent of Section 4 of the Mental Health Act 1983. There is no emergency admission procedure under the Mental Health (Northern Ireland) Order 1986.

Appendix 6

Amending legislation

Statutes

Children Act 1989
NHS and Community Care Act 1990
Courts and Legal Services Act 1990.
Criminal Procedure (Insanity and Unfitness to Plead) Act 1991
Criminal Justice Act 1991
Probation Service Act 1993
Mental Health (Amendment) Act 1994
Mental Health (Patients in the Community) Act 1995 ("the 1995 Act")
Health Authorities Act 1995
Armed Forces Act 1996
Crime (Sentences) Act 1997

Statutory Instruments

Legal Aid and Assistance Regulations 1989 (S.I. 1989/340)

Legal Aid and Assistance (Amendment) Regulations 1994 (S.I. 1994/805)

Mental Health (Nurses) Amendment Order 1993 (S.I.1993/2155)

Mental Health (Hospital, Guardianship and Consent to Treatment) Amendment Regulations 1993 (S.I.1993/2156)

Mental Health (After-care under Supervision) Regulations 1996 (S.I.1996/294)

Mental Health (Patients in the Community) (Transfers from Scotland) Regulations 1996 (S.I.1996/295)

Mental Health Review Tribunal (Amendment) Rules 1996 (S.I.1996/314)

Authorities for the Ashworth, Broadmoor and Rampton Hospitals (Establishment and Constitution) Order 1996 (S.I.1996/488)

Ashworth, Broadmoor and Rampton Hospital Authorities (Functions and Membership) Regulations 1996 (S.I.1996/489)

Mental Health Review Tribunals (Regions) Order 1996 (S.I.1996/510)

Mental Health (Hospital, Guardianship and Consent to Treatment) (Amendment) Regulations 1996 (S.I.1996/540)

Mental Health (Hospital, Guardianship and Consent to Treatment) Amendment Regulations 1997 (S.I.1997/ 801)

Mental Health Review Tribunal (Amendment) Rules 1998 (S.I.1998/1189)

Mental Health Review Tribunal (Region) Order (S.I.1998/1460)

Mental Health (Nurses) Order 1998

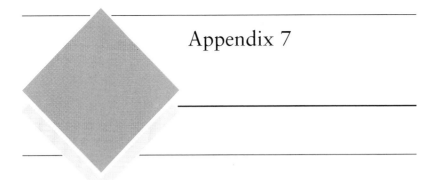

Appendix 7

Sentencing options

Post conviction pre-sentence

section 38 interim hospital order

Sentencing options for Magistrates' Courts

section 37 hospital and guardianship orders
section 43 committal to Crown Court
other criminal justice disposals include community order with conditions of treatment

For Murder

mandatory life sentence

section 2 offence Crime (Sentences) Act 1997

mandatory life sentence (sentence not fixed by law)
hospital and limitation directions under section 45A and section 45B may be attached

section 3 offence Crime (Sentences) Act 1997

mandatory minimum sentence of seven years
hospital and limitation directions may be attached (section 45A and 45B)
hospital order (with or without restrictions)

All other imprisonable offences

all appropriate criminal justice disposals
MH Act disposals - section 37 guardianship, section 37 hospital order (with or without restrictions under section 41), section 45A and B hospital and limitation direction

Criminal Procedure (Insanity) Act 1964

Where a jury has found the defendant unfit to plead or not guilty by reason of insanity, the full range of disposals under the Criminal Procedure (Insanity and Unfitness to Plead) Act 1991 are available, including a hospital admission order

Printed in the United Kingdom for The Stationery Office
J60558 9/98 C50 9385 9082